BEING

W

Shepherd Hoodwin

Summerjoy Press
LAGUNA NIGUEL, CALIFORNIA

BEING IN THE WORLD

Summerjoy Press
99 Pearl
Laguna Niguel CA 92677-4818

https://shepherdhoodwin.com
shoodwin@gmail.com

Copyright © 2016, 2020 by Shepherd Hoodwin

All rights reserved. No part of this publication may be reproduced, stored in a retrieval system, or transmitted, in any form or by any means, electronic, mechanical, photocopying, recording, or otherwise, without the prior written permission of the publisher, except by a reviewer, who may quote brief passages in a review.

ISBN: 9798606898893; Kindle: 9781885469182

Photograph of Shepherd Hoodwin by John Kilis.

Dedicated to

Stan Grindstaff

ACKNOWLEDGMENTS

My clients, for their questions and the use of session material.

Leslie-Anne Skolnik, Stan Grindstaff, and Pat Kendall, for editing.

Linda Scheurle, Fay Goldie, Seth Cohn, and Barry Carl, for transcribing.

Beauty is eternity gazing at itself in a mirror.
　　—Kahlil Gibran

CONTENTS

ACKNOWLEDGMENTS iv

PREFACE ix
   MICHAEL CHANNELING ix
   ORGANIZATION x
   EDITING x

INTRODUCTION xii

I A LIFE'S CONTEXT 1

1   THE GAME 2

2   LIFE TASK 10

3   COSMIC ORDER 25

4   MULTIPLE ASPECTS OF SELF 27

5   TIME 33

6   BEYOND TIME 37

7   BRINGING WHOLENESS 43

II THE LIFE CYCLE 51

8   INCARNATION 52

9   AGING 54

10   DEATH 57
   FEAR OF DEATH 57
   WHAT HAPPENS AFTER DEATH? 57
   RELATING TO THE INCARNATE 59
   BETWEEN LIFETIMES 60
   TIMES OF DEATH AND BIRTH 62

11   KARMA 63

WHAT IS KARMA? ... 63
WAKING UP ... 63
CHOICE ... 63
JESUS'S DEATH ... 64
VOODOO ... 64
MIND FUCK ... 65
BEING TRIGGERED ... 65
GRACE ... 65

III THE COLLECTIVE ... 67

12 ❧ GOD ... 68
UNIVERSAL CONSCIOUSNESS ... 68
DEFINING GOD ... 68
THE WAY ... 69
THE EVER-CHANGING GOD ... 69
IDENTITY IN GOD ... 69

13 ❧ RELIGION ... 71
WHAT RINGS TRUE ... 71
UPLIFTING THE BODY ... 71
PRAYER ... 72
RELIGIONS AND THE NEW AGE ... 73
STRUCTURE ... 73
LIVING SYMBOLS ... 73

14 ❧ INDIVIDUAL AND COLLECTIVE CONSCIOUSNESS 75
THOUGHT ... 75
KNOWLEDGE ... 75
THOUGHT CREATES ... 76
CHOOSING A TOPIC ... 76

15 ❧ GROUP ENERGY ... 77
MULTIPLICATION OF OPENNESS ... 77
BLENDING IN A GROUP ... 77
TRANSFORMING UNHEALTHY ATMOSPHERES ... 79

16 ❧ INTENT ... 80

17 ❧ PERFORMING AND ENERGY ... 87

IV CHANGING THE WORLD 90

18 ~ IMAGINATION 91

19 ~ CONTINUAL EVOLUTION 94

20 ~ RESPONSIBILITY 96

21 ~ THE ADOLESCENT CIVILIZATION 102

22 ~ PIONEERING NEW IMAGES OF REALITY ... 107

23 ~ BEAUTY 112

EPILOGUE 117

BACK MATTER 118

ABOUT THE AUTHOR 119

GLOSSARY 121

OTHER BOOKS BY SHEPHERD HOODWIN 123

REVIEWS 127

PREFACE

It has been suggested that we be in the world but not of it. Perhaps it is safe to say that most of us are in the world and of it. When I began my spiritual studies, I tried to be not in the world and not of it.

Everyone's path is different. There are those whose contribution to humanity is made through a more contemplative life. Being spiritual, however, does not necessarily exclude worldliness. Our loving and appropriate participation in the world, in whatever ways we feel moved, can contribute to its transformation.

Throughout history, there have been many visions for a better world. We can sense how beautiful it could be. Although enlightened activism is needed, it is the bringing forth of the beauty of our being that is the key to creating a beautiful world. This is *being* in the world. The more we resist the world, the more unpleasant it is for us, whereas the more we are truly in the world, the more beautiful we experience it to be. What better vocation is there than to bring the beauty of our being into the world?

I accessed the material in this book through channeling, working with a nonphysical entity known as Michael. Before reading it, you might find some background helpful.

MICHAEL CHANNELING

Channeling is a process of allowing a nonphysical intelligence to express through a person who is the "channel." It can be in words, energy, emotion, movement, and/or music, among other things. Michael is the name of a group or "entity" of 1,050 individual souls who have completed the physical and astral planes of creation, and teach from the causal plane. This is why they refer to themselves as "we." (They are not the same as the archangel Michael.) There are several Michael books by a number of other channels and authors who work with this same Michael group.

Most of the other Michael books deal with the Michael teachings, a complex and fascinating body of information about the way we set up our lives. *Journey of Your Soul: A Channel Explores the Michael Teachings* is my contribution thus far to that body of information. *Being in the World*, like *Loving from Your Soul*, *Growing Through Joy*, and *Opening to Healing*, does not cover the technical aspects of the Michael teachings, although it illuminates many of its principles. The few terms associated with the teachings are defined in the glossary.

ORGANIZATION

More than half the material in this book comes from lectures. The rest is from individual sessions. Some of the chapters are compilations of passages from various lectures and sessions. Most of those passages are in their own subchapter. If there are two or more different passages in a single subchapter, they are separated by asterisks. Questions and comments are italicized.

EDITING

When I channel, Michael makes use of the contents of my consciousness, and to some degree is limited by my limitations. Although this material is well beyond what I could produce on my own, it is also mine, and I take full responsibility for it. In general, I treated the original transcripts like first drafts, and polished them as I would my own writing—cutting, rearranging, and rewriting as necessary. Before publication I channeled Michael to get their modifications and "stamp of approval."

Being in the World presupposes we each are a soul who has lived other lives, but believing in reincarnation or even in

PREFACE

channeling is not necessary for an enjoyable and profitable reading of it. You can validate most of the ideas in it for yourself, and Michael encourages you to do so.

Sessions with Michael are clarifying, uplifting, and healing. May you experience this as you read their words, and feel more empowered to truly *be* in the world.

        Shepherd Hoodwin
        Laguna Niguel, California
        June 5, 2020

INTRODUCTION

The world is a place of great intensity and possibilities. The consciousness of each person participating in it now and in the past helped create its present state. It is the way it is because of your choices and those of everyone else, not because it is inevitable that it be as it is. On the other hand, if it could presently be a place of utopian harmony and peace, it would be. Obviously, consciousness has not thus far been high enough to permit this. However, anything is possible. The world is neutral; it can reflect any state of consciousness. Awareness of the vast possibilities of the world brings a desire to interact with it in the highest possible consciousness, so that the world of tomorrow will have a healthier origin.

Until now, humankind has been existing as if it were alone in the universe. However, new awareness of what is beyond has begun to emerge. The lectures and discussions in this book are designed to assist you in living from a consciousness that includes the greater whole. To change the world, it is necessary to change consciousness; if you change your own consciousness, you will inevitably affect the consciousness of others.

We support you on your path, and hope that the words on these pages invoke in you a vision that helps you walk more vigorously and effortlessly upon it.

Michael

Part I

A LIFE'S CONTEXT

1 ❦ THE GAME

Health is wholeness, and healing is a process of making something whole. There is no state of total wholeness except the Tao, the All That Is, in its primary, unexpressed state. Therefore, it is not possible to achieve ultimate health or wholeness on the physical (or any other) plane. Healing is the movement toward it, not its achievement. You cannot achieve perfect health or wholeness at some point and then freeze it. You can approach it, coming ever nearer to the goal, but you will never attain it until you finish the universal game and reunite with the Tao. This is one reason perfectionism is a neurosis—it is an attempt to freeze a state of wholeness.

There is nothing wrong with the fact that wholeness is unattainable. If you reached total wholeness by the end of this lifetime, what would you do after that? It is like completing a jigsaw puzzle. There is nothing left to do but start another one, which in the beginning will be totally incomplete.

The Tao plays in the seven planes of creation. The physical plane is the first. Since the Tao is whole, in and of itself, it must have a playground that is not complete so it can have the opportunity to do something. What is whole is in a state of equilibrium; it takes imbalance or incompleteness for there to be movement. For example, when you walk, you are off balance, falling forward, much of the time; when you are sitting, you are in balance.

The point of playing a game is not to complete it as quickly as possible. If that were your attitude, you would not begin it in the first place. You play because you want to play. Although it would be a bit much if the game never ended, you enjoy its duration. In fact, without an end, it would have no shape, so it would not be a game.

This universe is a playing board for the Tao, containing infinite smaller boards. As part of the Tao, we are all playing

THE GAME

a vast game, and smaller games within the game. Each has a beginning, a middle, and an end. You could say that the smallest game on the physical plane is a single day. There are various larger games that can take any number of daylong games to play. You could see every lifetime as a single game as well—it has a beginning, a middle, and an end.

Some feel that the end comes too quickly. If you are a contestant on a game show and the bell rings before you win the trip to Hawaii, that is the game! If you were always sure how the game would turn out, you would have no motivation to play it. However, there is always another game.

Every player helps create her games and agrees to play within their parameters. The games are not always easy, but they are ultimately fair, in spite of temporary unfairness along the way, because everyone is playing by the same rules.

The object of the largest game is total wholeness. Everyone will, at the end of it, reach this goal. In other words, everyone will be completely reabsorbed back into the Tao when he finishes the game. If you were to reach the goal now, however, you would miss most of the game.

Each of the smaller games within the larger game has its own object. For example, before every lifetime you choose a life task and see whether you can achieve it, or how much of it you can achieve.

You are not, in any of these games, actually competing against someone else. The whole idea of competition in this regard is illogical—you are part of the Tao, which is a unified whole. It is true that you are in the universe "pretending" that you are not whole so you can have new experiences and expand your wholeness. However, how can you compete when there is really only one thing?

Here is an apparent paradox. You are individual—you have a separate physical body. Yet what divides you from others? Can you really be divided from others? Could you exist without the presence of other human beings? Where does the skin of your body end and the air next to it begin? There is no space between your skin and the air. The most external molecule of your skin is adjacent to a molecule of air. They are only slightly different; they are made from the same elemental substance, expressed a little differently. It is rather like one color in a rainbow being adjacent to the next. If you move your awareness away from your skin through the molecules of air, you find another person, the Tao in a slightly different shape. Conveniently for you, the air molecules are transparent and lightweight. This allows the game piece that is your body to have flexibility of movement, which makes the game more fun.

The movement of your game piece moves the air and affects the other game pieces, and vice versa—in other words, you affect others, and they affect you. However, you are not in competition with them. During the game of life, you may think it is about "me against them," or "our team versus theirs." Apparent competition can sometimes challenge you to play your best, but when the game is over, everyone goes back to the same locker room.

You do not need competition with others to challenge you. You can "compete against yourself," as they say, which is not really competition, because when you win, no one loses; you are seeking the highest possible attainment for its own sake.

It is not a contradiction to seek perfection without being a perfectionist, without trying to have total perfection now. As with wholeness, total perfection exists only in the Tao, but the goal of perfection can motivate you to play the game as well as you can.

Many people play the game unconsciously. Let's say that you are competing in the Olympics in track. Track is a good example because it is an individual sport and is not competitive except in scoring—the activities are not in opposition to other players. In any case, you are not going to do the pole vault as well as you otherwise would if you are drunk. You might learn some things about it from attempting it drunk, but you are likely to ram into the crossbar. That is rather like playing the game unconsciously, without having your full faculties of alertness available. Often people's goal is to sleep as peacefully through the game as possible, occasionally using external substances to that end. Those who rock the boat are not usually welcome because it makes too much noise when people are trying to sleep!

More and more people, however, are realizing that they are playing a game. When that occurs, two things happen. One is that they play the game more seriously. The other is that they take the game less seriously: it matters, but at the same time it does not. This perspective gives you detachment and the ability to accept things as they are. You cannot do anything about the present score of the game—that is the way things are—but you can play your best game now. No one other than you is keeping score, but there are times when the game seems to be going better than others. There are days when you feel well and days when you do not. There are days when you win the lottery and days when you lose your job, but such events of themselves do not constitute winning or losing the game. Eventually, you *will* win. You cannot lose—there is nothing *to* lose, since you are already indivisible from the Tao, joined to all things. Winning a particular game is reawakening to that truth within a specific context through achieving understanding, joy, and love.

It seems that you are making light of the world's suffering by referring to life as a game.

There are, of course, games played purely for recreation. Even those sharpen skills. But perhaps you could think of what we are discussing here as being more akin to educational games.

The more skill one has, the more one's lessons come through joy. However, pain can help you learn to play the game more skillfully. It might be telling you that you are not playing the game in such a way as to bring pleasure. The pain is important but it is not the point; it is simply information. Let's say that you were driving and were not alert, so you had an accident and ended up in the hospital. Your pain gives you a vital piece of information—if you felt euphoria instead, it would be confusing. It would be telling you that when you play the game less well, you feel wonderful. So pain can be valuable from this standpoint.

You are not necessarily playing the game poorly now if you experience pain; in fact, sometimes pain increases when you are healing because buried problems from the past come to the surface. But as you increase harmony, you eventually reduce pain, which shows you that you are moving in the right direction. Resisting pain increases it. The more you accept pain, the more quickly you benefit from it.

If the Tao is complete, why does it want to play the game?

Completeness and incompleteness are two ends of one stick. Let's say that you build models and you have completed one. You might call that completeness perfection. All the pieces are now together and you know everything you want to know about that model from having gone through the process of constructing it. You may then wish to embark on a new model, something different that teaches you things you could not have learned from the previous model. The new model is incomplete but as you work on it, it moves toward completeness. Every time you complete a new model, you have expanded yourself.

The Tao is the part of all of us that has assimilated the lessons of the previous model, you might say. It is whole and complete. However, there are an infinite number of new models that could be built, each one potentially more sophisticated than the last.

The completeness of the Tao is one end of the stick; the

incompleteness of the universe is the other. Together they balance one another and allow for orderly progression. Everything springs from the Tao. If the Tao were not complete, there would be no stable foundation from which the incompleteness of the universe could spring, ultimately bringing a larger completeness. It is like a gymnast having an internal state of balance, allowing him to be unbalanced externally and bring new movement into that balance.

You are a dynamic part of the Tao. You are responsible for the Tao's expansion. You are not an imperfect little twerp crawling back to the Tao on your hands and knees, hoping that when you get there the Wizard will open the door and let you in. You are the means by which the All extends its completeness. All your experiences are new ones for the Tao. Their exact conditions have never existed before and never will again. New games allow for new understandings and different types of creativity. The Tao is the creator. Every artist seeks new forms of self-expression. If this is true of an individual, how much truer is it of the core creator? Being the All That Is without an opportunity to express itself would be like being a king with no kingdom; he would just sit in his castle. It would be boring for the Tao to stay the same for eternity. The universe is the way the Tao expresses itself and thereby avoids the boredom of "early retirement."

All things have consciousness, and all consciousness is expanding, even the consciousness of a blade of grass. By being what it is, it is gradually becoming more, thus able to express itself in larger, more sophisticated ways.

Virtually all people are at least partly asleep, somewhat functional but not fully aware. Awakening sleeping aspects of yourself is part of the game you are playing now. Living life asleep makes it harder. Sometimes athletes train by carrying additional weight; when they remove it, they are stronger and their task seems easier. Actors sometimes place marbles in their mouth to learn to enunciate; when they remove them, it is easier to speak with clear diction. When you remove the limitation of sleep, you live with more ease and power. Illusion and false personality [*see glossary*] are what cause consciousness to sleep. They function like the marbles and extra weight—they make it harder to play the game. The process of experiencing and then lessening and removing them strengthens your ability to play the game.

The ultimate object of the game is *agape*, or unconditional love. Playing the game expands the Tao, which *is* love, by giving it more opportunities for self-discovery. Encasing yourself in greed, stubbornness, or another fear-based pattern, and getting out of it, like Houdini getting out of a box at the bottom of a pool, gives you more consciousness of agape because you have vividly experienced what it is not. Expansion occurs through actions motivated by love, but the experience of being motivated by fear is not wasted—it contributes to your knowledge of love. You experience as much fear as you need to in order to see it clearly and awaken to love. Once you "get it," you transcend the polarity of love and fear; neither is an issue. You develop the capacity to simply be.

The game we, the Michael entity, play on the causal plane is not primarily about polarities such as love and fear, or positive and negative. We have already played that game, and have integrated both positive and negative into our consciousness. We therefore transcend polarities and almost completely experience the essence of things. You usually do not complete lessons about polarities on the physical plane. You continue them through the upper astral plane, where a new game begins. You could not begin a new game if you had not played the previous one.

Although the Tao has no beginning or end as you think of them, you could say that in the beginning the Tao built and completed one model. By now, it has completed several models. This universe is its current project. The Tao may later decide to do something other than building models. What that might be is beyond our ability to conceive, but it is the nature of a creator to create. How can a creator not create? At our core, we are each a part of the creator. We are also part of the creation. The creation part of us is becoming complete through the creator part of us playing the game.

Everything you create teaches you something about yourself because a part of you that was previously merely potential is now reality and you can see it. It is not merely a possibility or even a probability—it is there. When it is complete to your satisfaction, you can move on and create something else, building on your previous creation.

In playing the game, you draw from an infinite pool of possibilities. The way you play the game impacts which of those possibilities become probabilities, and which of those probabilities become realities. If the game you are playing is not as much fun at the moment as you would like, bear in mind that it keeps moving and changing. As you play the game the best you can now, you increase your pleasure and joy, at least eventually if not immediately. The better you get at the game, the more fun you have. This is partly why it pays to be on a true spiritual path; it helps you learn the rules of the game and improve your skills.

So have fun. Enjoy the game!

2 ❧ LIFE TASK

You are here on earth at this time because you chose to be. It is not haphazard or by chance. If you chose to come, you must have had a reason. The reason was probably not that you had nothing better to do. If that had been the case, you probably would have stayed where you were. The astral plane is less challenging, in certain respects anyway; it does not require you to deal with the severe limitations that are currently present on the physical plane, although some less-experienced souls are uncomfortable with the fluidity of the astral plane and tend to reincarnate as soon as possible after death.

In any case, you had your own reasons for coming. Do not assume that yours are the same as others'. You might wonder why someone else is not interested in spiritual or psychological teachings, for example. It is possible that these teachings are not relevant to her reasons for coming.

The physical plane is like a university at which the students are on independent study programs—they write their own curricula. They also grade themselves. There are resources they may take advantage of: teachers, libraries, laboratories, playing fields, auditoriums, infirmaries, and so on. Some go through the program at an accelerated speed; others are perennial students who look as if they will never graduate. Some are learning a great deal; others are going to parties every night. In a regular university, there tends to be criticism of those who take longer to graduate or those who prefer partying to studying. However, the university of the physical plane is neutral on the subject. It is just there, and people can use it in whatever ways they wish.

Do not assume that the choices one person makes about how he uses these resources are better than someone else's. If someone wishes to party and spend most of his time drunk or stoned, although that is not productive, it should not be assumed it is better to be productive than unproductive. You

LIFE TASK

may wish to associate with productive people—that is your choice. If people wish to be unproductive, however, or anything else for that matter, that is their prerogative unless they interfere with other people's right to choose.

Birds of a feather flock together. The party people tend to find one another, the studious ones tend to find one another, and so forth. You can find others at the university of life who want to have the same kinds of experiences you do.

You are not responsible for others. You might say, "Oh, but my friend here is going to fail if he doesn't study." Again, the program is self-graded. He may not consider it a failure. Even if he does, it will no doubt add to his education just as surely as an A+ would.

You are here for your own purposes. What are those purposes? How can you find out? You are usually most interested in those things that further your purposes, at least if you are reasonably in touch with your innate desires, which many people are not. Perhaps you have always wanted to help others but you do not even articulate that because you take it so much for granted. You assume that everyone else feels the same way if he is decent: "Of course, who would not want to devote his life to helping others?" Then, when you see someone who appears to be selfish, you shake your finger at him. If helping others is your passion, that is probably an indication that your life's work is connected with service. Anyone who is doing his life work will, at least indirectly, be serving others because he will be increasing the influence of universal love. Some people, however, focus more on aiding others directly, while some focus more on aiding themselves. Those in the latter group may also be helping others and those in the former may also be helping themselves, but the predominant thrust may be one or the other.

Those who have always felt a great urge to create something of beauty through the arts probably have that as part of their reason for coming. Likewise with those with an insatiable desire to learn. Learning may be through what you might call on-the-job training as well as through classrooms, books, and other media. Perhaps they felt frustrated after a number of lifetimes in which there were not many opportunities to learn and wanted to make up for lost time.

What if there is not any particular thrust at all, in terms of service, creativity, or study? Those are, after all, pretty highbrow; many people are not attracted to them. There are many, especially those with less experience on the physical plane, who are eager for any type of experience. They throw themselves into the drama of life and see what happens. Others are paying back karmas, and may find themselves in one crisis after another. Apparently, their lives are a mess. There are certainly ways that the negative impacts of karma can be softened through increased awareness, but karmic repayment may be their life purpose. Others may come with many agreements—for example, to bear children—and that is the main focus of their life. For others, the point of their lives may be to explore in depth a basic physical plane relationship, such as that of husband and wife, or a fundamental lesson, such as acceptance.

It may seem that their worlds are pretty small, and perhaps they are compared with yours. However, they may not like your world, or it may simply hold no interest. Let's say that you are in fifth grade and you are already reading adult books—you are precocious—and you have a sister in second grade. Would you tell your sister that she should be reading what you are reading? She probably could not even read books at the fifth grade level. The point of this analogy is to have acceptance for other people's paths. If you are a fifth grader who is reading *War and Peace*, you are not better than a second grader who is reading *Fun With Dick and Jane*. The second grader may actually be growing more by mastering that simple book than you are by reading *War and Peace*.

Here we are using an analogy where one path is

apparently more advanced than the other. People also judge others whose paths are just different. For example, scientists often think that their path is superior to that of religionists, that only cold, hard facts are going to solve problems and help humanity. On the other hand, religionists sometimes think that the scientists are deluded, that only religion will solve anything. Both paths have potential validity and can contribute to the progress and well-being of the whole.

Artists sometimes feel superior to others, and those who pursue modest occupations sometimes feel that their lives are less significant than those of people who make famous pieces of art. A famous piece of art is not the same, of course, as a great piece of art, and there are many ways art can be interesting, skillful, or pioneering. In any case, who can say for certain that one life contributes more than another? Every life is significant, and all such comparisons are meaningless. It is not useful to compare where you are on your path to where someone else is on his—they are different paths. The only comparison here that is useful is between where you are and where you wish to be—not to berate yourself, but to clarify your path.

In making such a comparison, be aware of unrealistic goals and perfectionism. Your purpose in coming is usually not defined by some material achievement, such as making a million dollars by the time you are forty, or becoming famous or successful in some way that is externally measured. You usually come seeking particular qualities of experience. To find them, you start from A and move toward B, but you probably do not care that much about B per se. There is a saying that it does not matter whether you win or lose, but how you play the game. Your life is a game and there is a goal, but the goal is there to facilitate the process of the game—it is to help you expand; it may not be intrinsically significant. Whether or not you become rich, famous, or otherwise outwardly successful, if you grow in love and understanding, your life has meaning.

For example, if you write beautiful poems but cannot get your work published, are you a failure? Through writing them, you may have developed greater compassion, insight, or resolution, as well as craftsmanship, artistic sensibility, or appreciation for the poetry of others.

There are those who do have as a life purpose achieving material success or fame, again not for its own sake, but for the lessons it brings. Those who achieve them can tell you that they are not the answer to all of life's problems. On the contrary, they tend to create a great deal of stress, which may be the point of achieving them: to have the opportunity to deal with those particular challenges. In any case, whatever the goal is, it is really just a way to define the process.

Before each lifetime, you, on a soul level, usually make a detailed life plan, which includes your task and how you intend to achieve it. Ample guidance is available to assist you in setting things up in a way that is likely to work. You can access the records of your plan intuitively or through a channel or psychic. However, they are not in English or in any human language. You do not generally operate in human language on the astral plane; you communicate telepathically at a level of thought beyond human language. Therefore, everything accessed must be translated. As with literature, two translations of your life task may look different but add up to roughly the same thing. Also, if your life task has many parts or if you have more than one, you might just receive a few pertinent highlights.

You probably really know what you came to do, at least to some degree and on some level. You may think that you do not because you are not able to find a career that feels like your life task. Many people, however, do not do their life tasks in their places of employment. Often life tasks do not require it or even permit it. If your task is primarily centered on relationships, for example, you will be in relationships wherever you are, so you may not require a specific career to complete your task. Work as a marriage counselor, for instance, might fit with your task, but it might not.

Few people achieve everything they set out to do in a lifetime. That is not a problem, just as it is not a problem if you do not get everything done on a particular day that you intended to. You do the best you can, and put off some things until another day.

Most people can tangibly work on an aspect of their life task in some way each day. If you are spending all your time just trying to survive and that is not your life task, you may feel frustrated, but even then you can have experiences and lessons that contribute to your task.

Is life task the same as life work, purpose, and plan?

These terms are sometimes used interchangeably but we could differentiate among them. Your life task is the primary spiritual accomplishment you seek, what you most want to explore—your overall reason for coming. Your life plan is your soul-level to-do list. It includes your life task as well as issues you want to work on, karmic repayments you've scheduled, agreements you've made with others, the possible timing of major events, and so forth. Life work is narrower than life task; it is the part of your task focused on a specific endeavor. Everyone has a life task, but not everyone needs a specific project through which to do it. True work is any occupation harmonious with your task and your essence in general. Life purpose is your motivation to do your task.

An example of a life task is fostering among others an awareness of the importance of world peace. It might impel a project such as writing a book or making a movie that inspires others to value world peace more highly. If that project consumes a great deal of that life's resources, it is the life work. There can be more than one life work, and simply learning to be more peaceful in everyday life, especially in challenging circumstances, may also be a vital part of the task. The life purpose, or motivation for the task, might simply be to help bring world peace. A person with that task might also have others, such as releasing a tendency toward playing the role of victim. He may also have as part of his life plan the intention to pay back a karmic debt to his mother.

Suppose that your life task is to build bridges between people of different backgrounds. One possible life work to achieve it would be to establish an organization that would help people in your multiethnic neighborhood get along better. If at one point you had the opportunity to do this but passed it up, for whatever reason, another feasible way to achieve your task may arise. Often there are many possibilities. If you follow any path you find fulfilling and are true to yourself, you are likely to end up achieving important parts of your life task. On the other hand, if you are full of sensings that you should do certain things, yet make choices that negate those sensings, you will probably not do your life task. For example, someone who longs to become a dancer but forces himself to become a doctor because his parents want him to is likely to have a sense of loss. Perhaps learning to be true to himself is actually his life task. In any case, if you clarify and follow your longings the best you can, you are likely to move in the direction of your life task. Your essence generally does a pretty good job of getting you at least in the vicinity of accomplishing it unless you resist a lot. You are more effective when you consciously cooperate with the process.

Let's say that you have had several lifetimes dealing with the issues of war and conflict resolution from many different standpoints. In this life, you want to integrate and apply what you have learned from having been a soldier, a civilian victim, a political leader, and so forth. If you are not conscious that this is your primary life task, you might simply experience a vague longing pushing you in that general direction. You might know that you feel strongly that there are better ways to resolve conflicts than what most people use, but it may not go beyond that. If you are conscious of your task, you are more likely to choose one or more ways to respond to your inner impulse. They might include becoming a negotiator or mediator, running for political office, working for the UN, writing a book, or volunteering for an organization that promotes citizen diplomacy. You might also choose a lower profile, dedicating yourself to demonstrating appropriate conflict resolution in all your interactions with others and perhaps being a mediator for your friends. Whatever you decide, when you hit upon a workable way to carry out your life task, your essence immediately sends energy through it and it feels right. You become excited about it. You start having more energy with which to live your life because you now have a lens that focuses your inner impulses in a specific direction. It is not that this is the only possible way you could achieve your life task, but it works.

If you choose a direction that is not in alignment with your life task but not too far off either, your essence exerts a magnetic pull, so to speak, drawing you into greater alignment with your task to help you get on course. Being in movement near your task is the key. In fact, any movement is preferable to none at all where the life task is concerned. We often urge people who are stuck to choose anything. There is much power in making a decision. Someone moving in the wrong direction, in the sense of doing something that goes against the grain, is more likely to turn around and move in a more satisfying direction than someone who is stuck—he has momentum. Fundamentally, all he needs to do is start listening to himself and adjust the "steering wheel" accordingly.

Sometimes you have a head-on collision that clearly lets you know that you are going the wrong way down a one-way street, so to speak. This should not discourage you from movement; it should only encourage you to turn around. After a while, your discernment grows. The direction that is the most harmonious with your life task usually feels the best. If it does not feel comfortable, you might still have a sense that you are accomplishing something you need to do, such as completing a painful relationship. Sometimes you do not validate its rightness until later. However, if it is painful and not yielding a sense of accomplishment, it is probably not your direction.

We suggest that you ask yourself often, "How does this feel to me?" If you are feeling happy in what you are doing, you are probably completing at least part of your life task. However, being honest with yourself is essential. There is no greater detriment to happiness than telling yourself you are content with things as they are when you are not. How do you really feel? You may not get the true answer when you first ask yourself, and may have to keep asking.

As long as you can feel that energy is moving well in your life, that you are taking steps that strengthen yourself and others, keep going in that direction. After a while, you simply choose a direction, know that it is right, and move with assurance toward its conclusion; then you pick another. It becomes as natural to you as breathing. Being a creative person, you choose something to create. You draw necessary tools toward you without too much trouble, find ways around obstacles, and every day move closer to completing it. Your focus is not on the completion per se, but on the joy of creating.

Some people have rigid ideas about their life work. If they cannot do a particular thing, they become frustrated and think they cannot do their life task. We suggest that you be flexible and do what is available for you to do. If you truly want to do that particular thing, put your heart and soul into it—you are capable of almost anything you can imagine yourself doing if you are willing to invest the necessary energy and resourcefulness. It is a question of whether a particular goal is worth the effort, which only you can decide. You are more likely to want to invest your effort for something that is in your life plan and that you are well suited for.

Saying yes to a particular goal means saying no to many others. You are on the physical plane partly to learn how to make choices. It is useful that life here is consecutive and you cannot do everything at once, compelling you to home in on choices. If you attempt to choose everything and spread your focus too thin, you are in effect choosing nothing because you will not have enough energy moving in any one direction to bring about what you are after.

Doing something that seems glamorous is not the point. Your life may look unglamorous by someone else's standards or even your own, but you have your own agenda, and if you are true to that, you will be content. Besides, lives that appear glamorous are often more ordinary (and harder work) than they seem.

Skillful choice-making, whether regarding life work or anything else, requires knowledge, thought, and creativity. If it could be reduced to a cut-and-dried formula, it would not be the major lesson it is. Some people adhere to simplistic rules such as "Always do what you want" or "Go with your gut feeling" so they do not have to think. Others overthink. The central way that engages all your faculties leads to the most satisfying choices. If you stay with the choice-making process long enough, exploring your thoughts and feelings about your options honestly and completely, a knowing will probably emerge in you that springs from your wholeness, rather than being an impulse from just a part of you. When you are deeply attuned to yourself, important decisions become easier, but they are usually not either mindless or purely intellectual.

Why can't you just learn everything on the astral plane?

There are many experiences that are not available on the astral plane but are available on the physical. The physical plane is an especially good place to learn about choices precisely because there is so much limitation. If you take a child to a large toy store and he can have any toy he wants, he may not be able to make up his mind—there is too much choice. But if there is a limitation—if you ask, "Would you prefer this one or that one?"—it is easier to learn about making choices. He has only two possibilities to weigh. When you become adept at choosing between two things, you can move on to choosing among three. With practice, you can see the relative benefits and disadvantages of ten, and then many more. By the time you are done, you can pick the most appropriate choice from infinity.

There are also many lessons related to the physical body's survival and death. This teaches much about life and agape. Acceptance of others is easier on the astral plane. The astral plane offers so much individual freedom that no one can really get in your way unless you allow him to. However, if you are in a situation on the physical plane in which it is difficult to love but you love anyway, you have learned that lesson well.

We do not wish to imply that the physical plane or any other plane exists merely for the education it promotes. It does do that, and that is a significant factor. The main purpose of the seven planes of creation, however, is to expand the Tao. It is like becoming an artist. In the earlier stages, you create less and study more. As you move along, you create more and study less because you now have skills. Another analogy is learning piano: if you cannot play scales, you are not going to be able to play a Beethoven sonata. If you are still learning the basics such as survival, you are not going to have much energy left for having an expansive, creative experience.

That is why we speak so much about lessons. It is not that lessons are important for themselves; it is that they help you move on to greater creativity. Even if you are at the level of playing scales, you can be creative and expansive in your scale-playing, but there is much potential beyond that.

There are educational opportunities on the physical plane that are not available on other planes. There are relationships that are not available elsewhere. On other planes, for example, you do not have mothers and fathers; you do not require them. By being born, you are utterly dependent on these figures. You learn surrender and how trust can be abused. You also have the opportunity to be mother and father, which teaches you nurturing and responsibility. Although there are no such things as mothers, fathers, and infants on the astral plane, issues of responsibility, caring, and so on are always relevant, although they manifest in different ways.

You are responsible only for yourself except in the case of a child or another who is literally dependent upon you for survival. However, your actions do affect everything else, even on the astral and higher planes, and learning to have the most beneficial impact possible is an important step toward agape. We could not do what we are doing on the causal plane if we had not had the experiences of the physical plane to prepare us. Being parent and child, for instance, taught us skills and insights we use in our interactions with you now.

How can we find out aspects of our life task pertinent to upcoming months? I have many choices in front of me right now, some of which seem to be better for me at the moment but in certain ways less interesting.

There are many resources available. Through meditation, you can more easily access your guides and essence, and can engage in dialogue with them about the various choices. You can also work with a psychic or channel. The key is to ask questions that zero in on what you wish to know.

There are many situations in which there is more than one good choice and it is simply a matter of deciding. Sometimes you are not ready to make that choice because all the factors are not clear. Work with the decision-making process until it feels complete. Usually at that point, you know what the best choice is for you. Although you need to make your own choices, speaking with someone who is detached such as a counselor, therapist, or friend can be useful; your essence, spirit guides, and teachers are not the only ones with worthwhile input. Seek input wherever it is available. However, if you are interested specifically in choices that will complement if not outright carry out your life task, it is useful to clarify your life task first.

If you make certain choices between lifetimes, do you ever change your mind once you get here?

Yes, but usually your life plan is not so specific as to be limiting. Let's say that your primary life task is to learn how to work with your hands and be of service to others through them. Being a repairman might be the life work you choose to carry out your task but there are many other means you could use. You usually set up your life to give you the opportunity to carry out your task in a variety of ways. Perhaps you choose a parent who is gifted with his hands and who teaches you many skills, giving you several options. If one does not work, you try another. You do not generally predetermine on the astral plane the specific physical tasks to which you will devote your life, such as becoming a repairman. You usually have some ideas in mind and may favor one more than others, but life is unpredictable and flexibility is necessary. For this reason, if you have a specific life work, you probably settled on it during this lifetime.

Let's say that at age eighteen you become fascinated with philosophy and, rather than working with your hands, you decide to get a doctorate in it. You teach it for the rest of your life, which facilitates your secondary life task quite well but not your primary one. You may put that off to another lifetime. However, that is likely to leave you feeling somewhat unfulfilled. Alternatively, you may find that you love whittling or making ceramics and do it as a hobby. You might give away your creations to people who are poor or in a nursing home as a form of service to others. You do your life task as a volunteer rather than through your career.

There are sometimes good reasons for changing your life plan. Let's say that you were too ambitious when you were making it and set it up to pay back several major karmas. During your life, you found that you were not as strong as you had thought. Therefore, you might have made a decision to put some of the karmas off until another lifetime.

Refusing to repay karmic debts out of false personality— in other words, out of avoidance and fear rather than a valid recognition that you took on too much—is a different matter. That is likely to leave you feeling frustrated and unbalanced. Often karma is so compelling that you complete it despite your resistance.

If you made these choices before a lifetime and you aren't consciously aware that you made them, how can you be consciously aware that you changed your mind?

You will not necessarily be consciously aware that you changed your mind but your life may change course. You might find your interests in life becoming different from what they were earlier or you might find yourself pulled to live in a different location.

When you are doing what you set out to do, your life is much more pleasing. This is partly because all the other people who have agreed to help you in your specific plan are then called into play. There begins to be greater synchronicity and depth to your life.

MEDITATION

Listen to the silence. Pull down from the shelf a book called

Life Tasks. Open it and find that it opens to a page that is particularly meaningful for you right now. Read it.

3 ~ COSMIC ORDER

Much of your life is amazingly well-ordered. Not only do you have a life plan but you make various arrangements ahead of time to help you complete it. Many of your situations are tailor-made for your needs. You are surrounded by people you have known in other lifetimes, some of whom you made agreements with to work together in a particular way.

We are not saying that life is governed by destiny or that everything is "supposed" to happen. Many things happen that are not part of your plan or that of others—there is a certain amount of chaos. However, there *is* a rhyme and reason for many of the things that come your way. Sometimes people try to figure out the reason behind a specific event when there is not one of great significance. More often, though, there is a reason that may not be seen. If you feel you are adrift in an ocean of chance, events that seem to confirm that view may arise, but even that is part of a vast order that could be defined by the statement, "You create your own reality."

Because the Tao established free will to expand itself, it is possible to violate the domain of others, causing pain. However, this is still contained within the cosmic order through the law of karma. Karma keeps energy in balance. Although karmas may be formed haphazardly, their repayment is governed by the cosmic order. Even non-karmic unpleasantness and unexpected setbacks that arise from time to time operate within the cosmic order.

Children are uncomfortable if they feel that there is a lack of order and reliability in their lives. In fact, this is true of all human beings to some degree. Those who are stuck in a bad situation may be acting partly from this need for order—they prefer the known to the unknown even if the known is miserable. One of the benefits of being on a spiritual journey is the opportunity to know that you are in the midst of a great, consistent, and reliable order. If you truly get this on a gut level, you will not find it so necessary that outer circumstances provide you with predictability.

It is said that only change can be counted upon. It is true that everything changes, but the cosmic order can also be counted upon. Those who are stubborn have a particular mistrust of the cosmic order. They tend to clutch the status quo like a drowning man hanging onto a log in the middle of the ocean. To continue the analogy, there is a big, beautiful yacht waiting to pick him up, but until he lets go of the log, he will not be able to board it. This is why letting go is often emphasized in spiritual teachings.

However, when letting go is discussed, often what you are letting go *to* is not considered. Some assume that letting go means becoming passive and doing nothing, but you are here to do something. The highest experience of letting go is to the cosmic order. It entails relaxing in the knowledge that there is one and that you are part of it. You can work with it in a way that gives you a sense of well-being. You may not fully know how to do this, but until you relax and let go of your mistrust of it, you have no way to learn.

If you are doing your best according to your present knowledge, the results occurring are currently the best available. If you do not like how things are working out, perhaps you need to learn more so that you can work with the cosmic order with greater success. For now, you can give thanks that everything that has worked out so far has done so based on the cosmic order.

4 ❧ MULTIPLE ASPECTS OF SELF

The complexity and beauty in a simple mineral is far more than what meets the eye. A plant multiplies that complexity many times, an animal many times more, and a sentient (self-aware) being such as a human, still many times further.

You are far more multifaceted than you realize. You have talents of which you consciously know nothing. You have done things that would boggle your mind. You do things now that would boggle your mind if you truly understood them. The particular aspect of you that you manifest in this lifetime and universe is perhaps about one twelve-thousandth of who you are. Your other aspects include past-life, probable future, and parallel selves, including the parallel and probable future selves of each past-life self. Your immediate, physical plane self is also amazingly complex, with many subpersonalities.

Although your focus now is physical, there are aspects of you on all planes and in the Tao itself. For example, your astral self, being closest to the physical, is directly involved with your physical self and often becomes your focus when you sleep. You have a causal self as well. It provides you with your core of understanding, the understanding beneath your understanding. You exist on all the higher planes as well.

Every part of you experiencing this planetary cycle comes together in your essence. Your essence, in turn, is part of larger and larger groupings.

You have experienced other planetary cycles, in different life forms, before this one, and you will probably experience other life forms in later cycles. These, too, are part of who you are and are available to you.

All this is orchestrated by your core self, the spark of the Tao; your experiences in the seven-plane universe are an expression of it and are included in it.

Even though your immediate self is a small part of your

wholeness, it is not insignificant. The reverse is true: you, in this particular lifetime and universe, are extraordinarily significant and large. Every part of the whole is valid; every part of the whole *is* the whole. In your physical body, every aspect contributes. If you were missing a fingernail, you would notice it. If you did not exist here, doing what you are doing, you as a whole would be incomplete.

This is partly why suicide is generally destructive not only to the personality but to the essence; the essence needs that part of self. When a piece of fruit is ripe, the tree is done with it and it comes off the tree easily. When it is not ripe, you practically have to rip it off. Likewise, when a lifetime is ready to end, it usually does so easily.

What you are is mighty but at the same time fragile. The way you treat yourself can be healing to your wholeness or subtract from its well-being. If you treat yourself with love and care, your whole self is showered with it. In addition, the love you give others spreads throughout their whole selves and onto others still. So what you do is important. Just as a vibrantly healthy cell promotes health throughout the whole organism, your healing helps heal the whole. Likewise, your successes promote success in the whole, and your increased understanding and love toward others and yourself contribute to the understanding and love of the whole. In fact, everything you do helps the whole move forward by bringing it new experience because there is no exact repetition.

Each person lives simultaneously in many parallel universes, where you are similar to who you are in this universe, to varying degrees, but in different circumstances, also to varying degrees. Your core traits remain the same, such as what we call in the Michael teachings your *role*, *overleaves,* and life task. Your essence creates these multiple realities to express itself fully and to explore alternative paths that look interesting.

Essence has certain things it wishes to do and learn, and

sends out impulses to all its relevant parallel incarnations. At least one parallel self will probably act on each of them. If, for example, you feel a strong impulse to learn to play a particular musical instrument but are not able to act on it, you probably will in at least one other universe.

If you do start to learn to play the instrument, you can draw on parallel selves who have already become successful in music, making it easier for you. You can also draw on your past-life (reincarnational) selves who were musicians; those selves you have been in other lifetimes are still present.

This is rather like drawing on the expertise of a family member. When you were in school, if a parent was a mathematician, you may have gotten some excellent help with your algebra. However, it is a more intimate experience because it is you. Such help is not a substitute for study with a teacher but it can make such study more productive, helping you polish or remember skills that a part of you already has.

To gain assistance from other aspects of yourself, simply be in an open state, ask specifically for what you need, and let yourself receive it. When people pray for help that does not come, usually the reason is that they do not adequately hold open the space in which to receive what is sought. In learning to play guitar, for instance, you could meditate, becoming relaxed and open, and then pick up the guitar and ask for assistance from the parts of you that have more skill in it. Quietly wait for an impulse and see what that impulse directs. You might find yourself improvising and able to do things you did not know you could.

Sometimes things you find yourself doing are in reply to calls coming in over the "switchboard" of your consciousness from other aspects of yourself that are asking for help. Maybe you find yourself having a strong urge to sit and be quiet or get some extra sleep. There are many possible reasons for such urges, but one is that you are sending assistance to another aspect of yourself. There is much value in taking time to be with other aspects of yourself in whatever way.

How does this vast cosmic view of yourself apply to the mundane problems of your daily life? It enables you to find the balance in which you understand that these immediate things are very unimportant and very important at the same time.

Life is full of dualities, opposites to be balanced, such as male/female, light/dark, and so forth. In uniting opposites, growth occurs. Importance/unimportance is another duality to be united. Each experience is important because it is an expansion of the Tao. On the other hand, as part of all you are doing, it is unimportant in that it has no real potential to dominate your total existence—you are too large. Even the worst conceivable thing that could happen would only be happening to a very small part of you. In this balanced view, you give everything your best and then don't worry about it too much. You know that if you do not succeed at something, you will later, if not in this lifetime, then in another lifetime or parallel. You do not waste your opportunities for practice and growth, but you are not driven by crisis either, exaggerating the importance of a single event.

Some people do not act unless they are in panic, so they create unnecessary crises. The more you act in your life out of the simple desire to act, the fewer crises come into your life—you are already doing what you need to do. You are self-motivated rather than externally driven.

Whenever you make the best choice you know how to make, you are in an upward motion. If later you look back and see that you did not actually make the best possible choice, that might indicate that you grew to the point where you could make a different choice—you now have greater understanding. That choice was part of your growth. In fact, every choice is a part of your growth, even the ones that are ill-conceived or unconsidered, because they all bring ramifications. As you understand those ramifications, you grow.

Being human is a difficult "assignment"; there are many potholes in the path you tread. Forgive yourself for the times you twist your ankle, stub your toe, or gash your knee. Do not judge them as wrong. They are teaching you many things, such as the ability to walk lightly with alertness. As you develop it, you bring to your wholeness a greater lightness and presence. In fact, everything you learn benefits your wholeness.

Do we sometimes go to parallel and reincarnational selves when we sleep, and do some of our dreams come from those meetings?

Yes, but you do not usually go to them in their physical realities. You meet them at the level of essence, the center of your being, and exchange thought. For example, let's say you are deciding between two jobs that both look good. While you "sleep on it," a parallel aspect of you chooses to do one job because it is more appropriate in that universe; you wake up saying, "I'm going to take the other job." This is a source of some of your dreams. More often, though, they are communications among aspects of your personality in this universe.

Can a reincarnational self be presently living on the astral plane?

Yes. After death, the part of personality based on the body's survival mechanisms ceases to be because it is no longer relevant, but the true personality remains as a sort of subpersonality of essence. As the lessons of that lifetime are completed, either astrally or in subsequent lifetimes, it is integrated into essence, just as a resolved subpersonality is integrated into your whole personality. At the same time, it continues to have experiences and grow as part of essence.

If you encounter a reincarnational self in past-life regression, chances are that it has not yet fully integrated into your essence. If you finish its lessons, it can then do so. You might be working with a cluster of several reincarnational selves to resolve a particular issue that came up in those lifetimes and is coming up again now. If you do not resolve it, you may join their ranks in a future lifetime, trying to help your future self resolve it. You tend not to remember fully integrated lifetimes because you are not working on them, although you might draw them in to remind you of strengths you had forgotten. Some people have hundreds of largely resolved past lives.

You are working with multiple aspects of yourself whether or not you are conscious of them. Becoming aware of them can vastly expand your perspective and resources.

[See chapter 31, "Parallel Universes," in my book *Journey of Your Soul* for more information.]

5 ❧ TIME

I understand that time doesn't exist, that everything is simultaneous.

When it is said that everything is simultaneous, it does not mean that everything is happening at the same time; it means that your essence is beyond time, so to your essence, all your lifetimes are simultaneously present. Again, that is not equivalent to all your lifetimes being at the same time, because your essence is not in time. You might say that at a certain level of development, your essence attaches itself to a particular point in time. Essence is like a plant going to seed. Each seed takes root in a different piece of ground (time). All of its seeds, however, exist simultaneously regardless of where they are planted.

Past, present, and future are simultaneous to your essence, but not to your personality, which exists in time. You have not experienced your future. Your future lifetimes exist, but as probabilities. If this is lifetime number 147 for you, from your vantage point you do not yet have the benefit of the experience of lifetime 148. Lifetime 148 is starting to take form in your projections, and you can work with it, but you cannot draw from lifetime 148 in the way you can from 146.

Time does exist and is valid within the confines of the physical plane, especially. Its influence is increasingly fluid on the astral and causal planes, and has no influence on the planes above them. An experience on the astral plane can be equivalent to the passing of a thousand physical years, but be "squeezed" into five minutes of physical time. Conversely, an experience there can be the equivalent of a second expanded into five minutes of physical time. Physical time relates to physical phenomena: the rotation of the earth and its orbit around the sun. Astral time relates to astral phenomena, what you might call the emotional or atmospheric movements of the earth. Astrally, time is softer;

it can be compressed and expanded. This is why when you dream it may seem as if you have been gone for hours when it has been only a few minutes in physical time. However, astral time is still connected to physical time; they are not divorced from each other. In general, time seems to travel faster on the astral plane than it does on the physical, although some souls experience it as being far slower.

Time is experienced differently on the lower, middle, and upper astral planes—the higher you go, the more elastic time is. You are usually on the lower astral plane between lifetimes. Because you are planning to come back for another lifetime, physical time is more of a factor. If, for example, you want to incarnate again in a particular year, you might compress your remaining astral activities into the amount of time you have.

Let's say that you died in 1923 and reincarnated in 1960. There were thirty-seven years between 1923 and 1960. During those years, you had much work that you wished to do in processing the lifetime you had just completed. There were also studies that you wanted to undertake before attempting another lifetime. In addition, you intended to take a "vacation" for twelve Earth years on Venus (in your astral body). Finally, you needed to come up with a life plan for your next lifetime and make the necessary agreements to carry it out. Being somewhat connected to the physical plane, you paced yourself so that you could get all that done. It was a reasonable amount to accomplish in that number of years if you were focused.

On the other hand, let's say that you committed suicide in 1923 and reincarnated in 1924 because you wanted to complete certain lessons with people who were still together. Had you missed that opportunity, you might have had to wait another three hundred years. So you had one year instead of thirty-seven, but you still had much to do. You wanted to explore the reasons you committed suicide and what you would need to do in your next lifetime to handle those factors

TIME

more successfully. In addition, you needed to do many of the things you would have done had you had thirty-seven years. If you were going to do that in one year's time, it would be an extremely compressed experience. Perhaps it was too much and you skipped some things. However, it is possible to have an amount of experience that would normally take several years on the physical plane in what correlates with one year on the astral.

For one thing, you are not limited on the astral plane by physical plane necessities: you do not have to stop to eat three meals a day. You do not need eight hours of sleep. There are periods of rest and regeneration, but these are flexible. You do not have to earn a living. You can just play for twenty thousand years if you wish, and it may go by quickly if it is not a very compressed experience. Most people take lengthy breaks from incarnating on the physical plane at times. That period may be spent visiting other realities, studying the akashic records (the universal "library"), or working as a spirit guide for people on the physical plane. There are many other alternatives as well.

When you are finished with the physical plane and are no longer coming back to it, you move to the middle astral plane. Here, physical time becomes a more distant concern. You do not need to pace yourself according to it as much.

On the upper astral and causal planes, the influence of physical plane time is more distant still. Causal time relates to causal phenomena, or the intellectual movements of the earth. Changing thought marks the passage of time.

We, being causal, can relate to the physical plane in a variety of time frames. A progression to us is not necessarily a progression that you would think of as chronological, although it is logical to us—logical but not chronological. Our experience is not linear; it is multidimensional. That is actually the case on the physical plane as well, but it is less obvious. You experience many things at the same time; you are simply not conscious of all of them at once.

The high planes (the mental, messianic, and buddhaic) are timeless. They deal with the essence of things. They do not relate to any source of periodic divisions whatsoever. The mental plane is the source of pure thought. The messianic is the source of pure emotion. The buddhaic is the source of pure energy. They differentiate the Tao's expression of itself into the universe. The akashic plane connects the high and low planes and provides a resource for all of them.

It is the very rigidity of the physical plane, including its time, that provides its unique lessons. It also can tire you after a while, and the astral plane can offer a welcome break. However, many people cannot handle its fluidity very well; they need and even desire the rigidity of the physical. If you end your physical plane cycle prematurely, you may have trouble, because if you do not master the rigid structure, you may be at sea in a more flexible one. It is like the need to develop discipline within a set of rules before you can bend or break them. A composer of music who knows the rules and then breaks them or invents new ones is more effective than someone who never knew the rules at all.

6 ❧ BEYOND TIME

Although time is useful, it tends to be more of a control than is necessary. Time is rather like the lines on a piece of graph paper that an architect might use in designing a building. The little boxes formed by these intersecting lines help the architect keep track of his various design choices. He could sketch his design without this measured structure, but it helps him to be more accurate, which is especially useful if he is not highly experienced. When the building is built, however, there are no horizontal and vertical lines in the sky behind it.

Similarly, time helps people organize their experiences, taking them one at a *time*. However, even on the physical plane, everything has an existence beyond time—it exists timelessly in the present moment. While you are carving a sculpture, for instance, its progress is measured against time: it takes so long to do, and it may relate to other events occurring at the same time. Once it is completed, however, it is beyond time—time is largely irrelevant to it; the sculpture simply is. It is true that the earth is still orbiting the sun and rotating, but that fact does not directly affect the sculpture at this point. Of course, if it is outside, the sun, wind, rain, and other elements may wear down the structure over time, but it is not time that wears it down; it is interaction with the elements.

You create your life against the lines of time. They are convenient. If you know that a meeting is at a certain point on your graph and others agree on that way of looking at reality, you can all converge at that point. However, your entire being is not limited by where you happen to be in physical reality on either the time or space continuum (space is another graph). A small part of you appears to be conforming to the dictates of this structure, but the larger part of you is doing a variety of other things.

For instance, you are always in dynamic communication

with many other souls. You may not be consciously aware of this, but you would be aware of it if such communication halted. There are those who experience less such interaction than others, by reason of their emphases in life. Their experience of life is different because of this.

Here are some rudimentary illustrations of this communication—perhaps you have had these experiences: You think of someone you want to call, and moments later, he calls you. You feel a pain in a particular part of your body and later learn that someone you are close to had a pain in the same area at that time. You get an idea for something new and do not act on it; then someone else comes out with the same thing; you and that other person were in touch with the same source but did not know it consciously.

When you have dreams at night with continuing casts of characters, you are probably meeting friends who are not physical or who are physical somewhere else and are communicating with you. In the world of space and time, you may be in your bed from 3:00 to 3:05 a.m., but your experience is not predominantly in your bed, and may seem like hours. Conversely, an experience that spans hours may seem like minutes. Of course, you may not remember the experience at all consciously, but there is much more to you than what is conscious.

This can be demonstrated in many ways. Under hypnosis, people sometimes speak languages they do not know consciously, describe locales they have never been to, accurately predict future events, and so on. In therapy, you may discover subpersonalities that have been influencing you without your knowledge. While speaking to a friend or a group, you might find yourself saying things you did not know you knew but which impress you with their substance and meaning.

The point is that a human being is a very large thing. You are not limited to where you happen to be in the world of space and time. When you look at your schedule, think of that! Think of all you will bring to your seven o'clock appointment, how large you are and how many other beings you are touching in any moment. You may not do much differently, but if you ground yourself in this larger consciousness, you will see your life differently. For one thing, you will see yourself not as time's prisoner but as its creator.

In fact, you did help create time. You and many others set up this time frame in which to play this game. It is part of the game board and facilitates the playing, but it is really not so important. Time structures are, by definition, limited—a year is 365 or 366 days—but time itself is in endless supply. It is a circle that keeps turning, that does not end even at death. Forms keep changing but you never actually run out of time, or space for that matter. You can accomplish in another time structure what you do not in this one.

You are here partly to learn to make the best choices you can. Time is helpful in teaching this. It gives you some limitations to work with. For example, from three to five o'clock you can do A, B, or C. This is easier to handle than choosing from all eternity and all possibilities. In time, only certain choices come to you at once.

If you feel that your choices within the confines of time are too narrow, maybe you can do something about that. There may be some larger choices you can change to free your time. Others complain that they have too much time; they are probably drifting rather than making choices. In any case, we would recommend that you not take time quite so seriously. You live in eternity right now. People think that only after they die will they experience eternity. Eternity is the present moment. It has no beginning and no end. You never stop being.

Why is it that in Mexico, if you make an appointment for six o'clock, people show up at eight or nine o'clock?

One reason is that in more affluent countries, there is often a desire to pack many activities into one's life. It requires much precision with time to fit them in. When there are fewer things to be busy with, being on time has less significance. There are advantages and disadvantages to having life so structured. The ideal is to have adequate structure to allow for the experiences you want to have, but not so much that time becomes a dictator, which it has for many in affluent nations.

The ability to be precise in relationship to time is useful. People who do not understand time and have no ability to work within its boundaries are at a disadvantage in playing a game that has time as one of its main elements. However, the goal in all things is to find balance. While Americans may be appalled at Mexicans' casualness about time, Mexicans may be just as appalled at Americans' sometimes excessive concern about punctuality. Each culture can learn from others.

People do many things automatically or assume them to be necessary, but you can make choices about how you spend your time. Ultimately, you have control over it. For example, you may assume that your job has to be forty hours a week, eight hours a day, five days a week, because that is what everyone else does. However, you might be able to negotiate a different arrangement that suits you better, either fewer or more hours, or the same number in a different schedule. Perhaps you do things during your day that you could pay someone else to do, or you pay someone else to do things that you would find balancing to do yourself. If you want to spend time with someone and find that you do not have the opportunity to share an entire afternoon, perhaps you could include him in something else you are going to do anyway. If you are supporting a lifestyle that you really do not care about and are willing to have a smaller place to live, an older car, or none at all, you could do things with your time that do matter to you.

There is no right or wrong way to use your time. However, the more conscious you are of it, the more able you are to use it creatively, resourcefully, and in alignment with your true purpose for being on earth. Your life gives you endless opportunities for this, but you will not take advantage of them if you are asleep on your feet. The hallmark of a truly spiritual person is wakefulness, seeing and engaging with what is. The person who is asleep does not see what is. He lives out his life according to precepts: "Of course, this is the way to be." "This is what my father or mother did" or conversely, "This is the opposite of what my father or mother did." He does little thinking about the things that are most important in life: "What do I truly want?" "Why am I here?" "How can I contribute most to my own growth and the growth of others?" "What do I need?" "Who am I?" The more asleep a person is, the more he will assume that these answers are givens. "Of course, I go to church every Sunday. This is what a good person does." People who are asleep do not like to be prodded or questioned, and it is not necessarily your business to question them. People wake up when they are ready, when being asleep is more uncomfortable than waking up.

In wakefulness, the more knowledge you have, the better choices you are capable of making. The more you understand why you have done the things you have done in the past, the freer you can become from old influences. We are not suggesting that you undergo endless self-analysis; some people become trapped in that. This type of knowledge comes from observation. You observe most accurately from a still place. Have you ever gone to an art gallery or museum and really looked at one piece of art? Sometimes it is difficult, isn't it, to quiet your intellect and really see what is there. Artists sometimes wring their hands at the way others observe their art, giving it a cursory glance and interpreting it in light of past conditioning. It is, at first, harder work to approach a work of art without assumptions but it is far more rewarding. If you look at your life with fresh eyes, you will also find it far more rewarding. The more awake you are, the more you can deliberately create a pleasing reality.

There is really just one moment: now. The past and future exist now. You can change the past as well as the future now. You are a fluid, vast, extraordinarily powerful being. You have chosen to express yourself through a relatively finite physical body that functions in relationship to the limitations of the Earth's orbit and rotation. The more you know that you are that force behind and beyond your body, the more powerful and limitless you will know yourself to be.

7 ❧ BRINGING WHOLENESS

You are a whole yet part of something greater, just as each organ of your body is a whole yet part of you. The effectiveness of any whole depends upon how compatible the parts are. When the parts of your body work together compatibly, there is health. Healing is restoring the compatibility of the parts with the whole.

One larger grouping of which you are a part is the human race, which is a collection of smaller wholes. It is not realistic to expect world peace until there is compatibility among and within the smaller wholes that comprise it. The smallest whole is an individual human being, which is contained within larger wholes such as family and community.

The atmosphere of a whole is what allows it to be greater than the sum of its parts. Compatibility helps create atmosphere. Compatibility is not generated by some individuals dictating to others. It arises from each part finding its true function. Again using the analogy of your body, your heart and lungs are compatible when each is being true to itself. By contributing who you are to the whole, you make possible a larger compatibility. The fact that political change is increasingly occurring with relatively little violence suggests that more people are beginning to understand the importance of their individual contributions and those of others.

The whole reflects the parts and the parts reflect the whole. Dictatorial governments reflect dictatorial dynamics within and among individuals. Likewise, dictatorial dynamics within and among individuals reflect dictatorial leadership. If there is enlightened leadership, an atmosphere can be generated that supports individual growth. Nevertheless, it is unlikely for such enlightened leadership to emerge until there are enough individuals who can support its presence by creating an atmosphere conducive to it. Your support for more enlightened leaders is meaningful because it contributes to such atmosphere. Part of the reason, incidentally, for group meditation before channeling is that it helps build a collective atmosphere. Channeling cannot happen effectively in a vacuum.

If you wish to be effective in anything you do, create an internal atmosphere based on the compatibility of the various parts of yourself. Before you set out to work on any task, allow your atmosphere to come together. This may simply mean pausing for a moment and listening to yourself. It may mean organizing your thoughts or tools, or doing some planning. Make sure that you agree with yourself as to what you want to do. You are less effective if you are on automatic pilot.

Increasing your inner compatibility and your compatibility with others begins with recognizing the validity of each part, that it has a function and purpose. It is not a question of eradicating anything or anyone, but of integrating and evolving all the parts.

Hitler believed that he could create a perfect race by eliminating certain parts of the whole. He epitomized the consciousness of eradication, but in fact most people are trying to get rid of some parts of themselves or others. When these parts are instead integrated, they often turn out to be the key factors in allowing what needs to happen next to occur. When they were repressed, they were the missing links. For example, if you integrate your anger rather than suppressing and trying to eliminate it, you find that it becomes transformed into an important part of your power.

Sometimes children in a classroom are disruptive. Wise teachers recognize the special contributions such children can make. Often, through love and acceptance, teachers can help actualize that potential.

You may choose not to have certain people or things in your life. That is your right. Perhaps you recognize that they do not belong there. Every part, however, belongs somewhere, in some form. You cannot determine where another part belongs; you can only determine where you belong and what belongs in your space. However, it is sometimes a good idea not to be too quick to decide: a person to whom you initially react negatively may become an important friend or ally once you work through what is bothering you.

Similarly, if instead of trying to get rid of feelings and thoughts you do not like, you mine the gold in them, they can stimulate unexpected revelations and bring you great growth. If you try to insulate yourself from them, you will not attain wholeness.

You could define an enlightened person as one who has complete acceptance and therefore has no need to try to eliminate anything; rather, she seeks to integrate and transform. As a result, she is comfortable in any situation. Acceptance does not imply inaction or a lack of boundaries. An enlightened person may act to stop violence, for instance, not because she judges the feelings behind it but because expressing them in a way that harms others is inappropriate. Judgment seeks to eliminate something, whereas love includes. By including the person committing the violence in her love and compassion while stopping his violent actions, she offers the violent person a place to heal those feelings. Accepting all of your feelings is the beginning of integration; judging and trying to eliminate some of them keeps you fragmented.

Often people do not love their body. They may not seek to eliminate it but they do not fully accept it either. Suppose that you own a business and have an employee who does his job very well but is not pleasing to your eyes. You would not think very much of yourself if you criticized him for not conforming to your idea of physical beauty. Yet many people think nothing of withholding love from their body because they judge it as not being beautiful. When you think about the remarkable things your body does for you day by day, your view may shift. Your body may just be a scapegoat for something within you of which you are critical. If that is the case and you find out what it is, you may no longer see your body in the same way.

MEDITATION

Close your eyes and go through your entire body, a part at a time. Thank each part for what it does for you, and do what is necessary to make peace with it. If you have judged it as not being beautiful or good, ask it to forgive you. Then visualize every cell of your body receiving love, healing, upliftment, or whatever else you specifically wish to send it.

Those who are consistently peaceful and joyful know how to handle pain. Despite a common belief to the contrary, you can have joy in the presence of pain (and vice versa). There are those who experience a certain level of well-being because their existence has not been very troubled. However, there can be a higher level of well-being in those who have experienced pain and know what to do with it.

When you include pain and the lessons it brings, not only is it often reduced or even eliminated but you become more whole. Your pain may have been there simply to remind you to include a part of yourself in your wholeness. When you do, you may not need it anymore. Your primary goal wasn't to eliminate pain, but you did eliminate it by including it.

Joy and pain is a polarity that needs to be united. Another such polarity is higher self and lower self. People on the spiritual path consider their higher self to be good; as a result, they try to include it. On the other hand, they may consider their lower self to be bad and attempt to exclude it. However, you cannot fully include your higher self without fully including your lower self because they are both part of your wholeness. Your lower self allows you to experience your higher self in your body. Furthermore, when you do not include your lower self, its pain stays with you. When you include it, it begins to heal.

What about Jesus apparently saying that if your eye offends you, pluck it out, and if your hand offends you, cut if off, rather than your whole body dying?

Your eyes have to do with perspective or attitude and your hands with action. He was likely suggesting that if you have an attitude or approach that is not working, it is better to let it go. If you stubbornly hold onto it, you become sick. The most effective way to let it go is to include it in a larger, loving context so that you can truly see and transform it. If you deny or repress it, it is still around. Jesus was speaking of the well-being of the whole.

If you find someone offensive, how can you end your relationship with him if you're not excluding offending parts?

Choosing not to spend time with someone is not the same as invalidating him. You can have unconditional love for someone, appreciating his value as part of the whole, while creating the right distance for yourself. As long as you remain in a relationship with him, you may be filling a space that might be better filled by someone else who can valuably interact with him. In finding your right place, you are helping those around you find theirs as well.

Like attracts like. As you become a more loving and inclusive person, you tend to attract others who are likewise. There is no need to hang onto those who are not. It is not your duty to save or change them. Trying to change others is not inclusive of who they are.

On the other hand, if they trigger upset in you, you might want to examine the reasons before you are too quick to end your relationship with them. When you have total acceptance for all the parts of yourself, you have total acceptance for others and they do not trigger you. Acceptance is seeing the worth and validity of each part, its right to exist. When you try to eliminate something in yourself or in others, it is repression. The ultimate embodiment of repression is suicide or murder. When there is right relationship with all the parts of the whole, each part can blossom.

Offensive characteristics are only a part of the whole person. If you are going to appraise someone fairly (including yourself), you must be able to see him as a whole. When you are being triggered, you tend to see the offensive traits out of proportion.

How can you accept something such as prejudice?

Prejudice is a good example because it itself excludes. If you seek to exclude it, there is even more exclusion. It can be appropriate to speak out about such things and to do what can be done. An approach that is not exclusive is to shed light, to do your best to inspire in those listening a sense that each part of the whole is valid and necessary. Excluding those who are doing the excluding, making them wrong, creates more separation. Judging prejudiced people isn't helpful. The point is to do what you can to bring change.

Everyone has free choice. If you choose not to buy a particular country's products until it changes a policy, that is a valid choice. If you do not wish to be in a relationship with someone as long as he is drinking, that does not necessarily imply that you think he is bad or are trying to change him—it is simply an expression of your choice.

It is worthwhile to consider how you approach bringing change. If you see others as enemies to be fought, they tend to act as if they are. If you see them as being on your side and seek to bring added light to the situation, they also tend to reflect that view. Everyone may not actually be on your side but everyone is in the same boat.

Those who see enemies all around them have many inner enemies, many battles going on within. If you are interested in peace, the place to begin is in how you approach your own life. If you are not doing something the way you might like to, do you battle yourself about it? Are you your own worst enemy? Or in loving acceptance, do you shed light on the subject? The action you take might look similar in both cases but the intent makes all the difference in the world.

For example, if you wish to lose weight and you see yourself as your enemy, you will battle and judge yourself when you eat things you think you should not. If you see yourself as your most loving friend, you view what you are doing inclusively, with love. You shed light on your eating choices so you can change them, if need be. If you battle something, it runs from you; if you embrace something, it is drawn to you. You cannot heal and transform something that is running from you.

If parents treat their children as enemies, the children tend to run from their authority. Parents who see their children in terms of good and bad often create bad behavior in them. Those who see their children as being on their side and include all their behavior as being for a reason generally have much less difficulty with them. They seek to shed light on their children's occasional misbehavior rather than punishing it. The whole attitude of punishment for misdeeds, so pervasive in the world, reflects a deep polarization between good and evil that perpetuates the battle.

Increase light as you are able. When you battle something, you are saying that it is bigger than you. When you try to eliminate it, it is because you believe that it has power over you. When you judge it, it is because you feel that it must be kept away from you. When you identify with wholeness, there are no threats. Therefore, you do not need to eliminate anything. When all your inner parts are free to work together compatibly, you are effective and peaceful, bringing peace to others and experiencing oneness with all things.

Part II

THE LIFE CYCLE

8 ❧ INCARNATION

There is almost always a soul willing to incarnate into a body, even if it is unhealthy, as long as it can sustain life.

Each parent usually has his or her own child agreements with various souls. If the couple has more than one child together, they usually take turns honoring their agreements. Although the parents may decide on an essence level even before conception who will incarnate as their next child, such arrangements are subject to change as circumstances change—the whole situation must be considered.

When does the soul enter the body?

Incarnation—the soul joining permanently with the body—most often occurs at birth with the first breath. However, it is not unusual for it to occur up to three weeks before birth. Incarnation may also occur up to four weeks after birth if the child is being adopted and it's uncertain whom the parents will be. Rarely, it occurs as early as three months after conception. Souls who incarnate that early wish to have the whole physical experience of being in the womb, particularly those who are fairly new to the physical plane.

What happens if a fetus is aborted before it is born? Does that count as a lifetime for the soul?

If there is a possibility of an abortion, miscarriage, or stillbirth, usually the soul, being sensible, waits to incarnate. It does not count as a lifetime unless there is incarnation.

The soul does tend to spend time near a fetus that will likely become its body, keeping an eye on it. Pregnant mothers instinctively feel its presence as well as the extra care of her spirit guides. Some souls are present at conception. Many hover quite a bit early on in the pregnancy. More experienced souls tend to have less interest in the fetus as long as it is progressing in a healthy manner, although they still have a relationship with it. In any case, the soul's presence is stronger seven or eight months into the pregnancy.

If some souls don't incarnate until after birth, how would they be able to have birth trauma?

There is a connection between the soul and the fetus well before incarnation, just as there is a relationship between partners before marriage. The incarnation "ties the knot." The soul chooses its body and begins to imprint it with its energy once it knows that it will probably incarnate in it. So what the body goes through, even prenatally, is likely to relate to issues that the essence is dealing with. By the same token, the soul is affected by the body's experience.

Your body and soul both contribute to your personality. Even if the incarnating soul is a last-minute replacement whose first contact with the body is after birth, the trauma is there in your body and therefore in your personality.

9 ❧ AGING

There is value in experiencing aging. You have aged in human bodies many times. One lesson of aging is freedom from excessive attachment. If there is acceptance of things as they are, a seventy-year-old who cannot do things she did ten or twenty years earlier has the opportunity to let go of having to do those things: if she cannot do them, she cannot do them. The alternative to acceptance is inner struggle. Any kind of physical disability teaches the same lesson.

Some people have lessons about not being considered as attractive as they grow older. However, people are generally most comfortable with others in their age range because there is greater compatibility, although there may be excitement and fascination with what is different. It is similar to differences in body size. A body that is six-foot-five and weighs two hundred fifty pounds tends to feel awkward with a body that is five-foot-two and weighs one hundred pounds, even if intrigued by it. The needs of the personality or soul can supersede those of the body, and there are often good reasons for that to occur. For example, someone in an older body might have a mate agreement with someone younger. However, older people who look longingly on those who are much younger, wanting to be attractive to them, are usually insecure or stuck emotionally in the past.

Although growing old does bring certain limitations, it is not necessarily synonymous with a loss of vitality. There are people at seventy who have as much vitality as when they were thirty, or even more. They generally live balanced lives. Usually they have work or activities they enjoy, but do not overwork. They enjoy good food, but not too much of any particular kind. They exercise regularly and well in ways that are appropriate for their bodies. And they may have fulfilling sexual relationships, which can be quite youthening to the physical body. They generally look younger than their years, but they obviously do not look as if they were thirty even if they have the same energy level as a thirty-year-old. They may end up living another twenty years or more, or they may feel finished with their lives and die, usually peacefully and without much fanfare. Such a balanced life is usually not possible for someone who is repaying a great deal of karma. Karma tends to keep you off-center and be draining for your physical body, if not eliminating it altogether.

One sure way to experience diminishing vitality in your life is to see life as a burden to be borne. Many people see their lives as consisting of one problem after another, and for some, this is their actual experience. All lives are not the same in this regard, although some people see their problems as being larger than they are, whereas others take them in stride. Seeing one's life in terms of problems can get to be a habit as a defense against further difficulties. The attitude might be, "I don't dare let down my guard for a moment or another problem will attack me." That does not actually help. If there are many problems in your life at a particular time or throughout your life, you can acknowledge them and work on them, looking for solutions. Bracing yourself against them, however, is likely to create more problems.

Those who maintain a high energy level late in life are not necessarily exceptional or highly spiritual people. They usually do have a bright and positive outlook, and a sense that their lives have value. In addition, they are usually blessed with a naturally strong constitution—good genes, as they say. On a soul level, you chose your genes along with everything else. If you chose a weaker constitution, you might be working out some spiritual issues in your body, or you might have chosen your body for other reasons and a weak constitution was part of the package—there are many reasons a person might choose a particular body. However, whatever type of constitution you have, it is worthwhile to change the belief, if you have it, that as you get older, your vitality must decrease. Beliefs can become self-fulfilling prophesies.

10 ❧ DEATH

The manner in which you die is one of the most important choices you make. If you die well, your death can be a blessing not only for yourself but also for those around you.

FEAR OF DEATH

Your body is programmed to survive. The fear of death largely springs out of its survival instincts. You need this natural mechanism. If you did not have a certain level of survival instinct, you would lose reflexes that protect you in dangerous situations. Your experience of this instinct, however, can be transformed. If you are living with alertness, it is not necessary to have an attack of fear to motivate you to be careful. If your body begins to trust that you as its occupant are going to take good care of it, it can relax on an instinctive level.

It is helpful to realize that you have had many bodies before, and may have many more in the future. Death is not the end. Although a number of your deaths were no doubt traumatic, you have also had many easy, peaceful passages. Death does not have to be traumatic.

Any fear you face is lessened. If you recognize and accept whatever fear of death you have, you can reduce it if it is getting in the way of living freely. You might try vividly imagining your death, making friends with it. You can also reduce your fear of it by working with both your painful and pleasant past-life deaths through regression.

WHAT HAPPENS AFTER DEATH?

Those who have lived more consciously tend to die more consciously. They are likely to be ready to move on to the next step almost immediately, whatever that proves to be.

Most souls greet their loved ones shortly after passing over. People's guides create whatever environment will be most comfortable for them. Someone who loved parties might be welcomed by a party, for example. After people have adjusted, their guides offer them a variety of activities. Often they continue with what they were doing before they incarnated. Some souls like to travel between lives. Others take advantage of various educational or research opportunities. They may become a spirit guide and/or work for the benefit of humanity in other ways, such as working with healing energy.

Someone who believes in heaven and hell might experience one or the other after death. On the astral plane it is relatively easy to create your image of reality. Other souls might play along with it for your benefit but the show has little depth to it. If a person is full of guilt and shame that needs to be cleansed away or at least acknowledged, creating "hell" might be useful temporarily. Its monsters are symbols of what is within.

Although most people find death to be a liberating experience, those who lived with a lot of false personality are more likely to die in turmoil or confusion, especially if they created major karmic ribbons. They may try to maintain their blinders but cannot entirely, because there is less support for false personality on the other side. Or they may have remorse for things they did and go into isolation for a while to come to grips with them. Although "all is choice" and no one can be forced to face whatever was not faced while incarnate, doing so is encouraged, and some time alone can be helpful as the fear-based illusions of the physical plane fade.

Most souls in a coma leading to death leave the body at the onset of the coma and maintain conscious awareness on the astral plane, but some are overwhelmed. If the event that led to the coma was traumatic, such as a brutal assault that the person wasn't equipped to understand and handle, the soul may be "out of it" to some degree and may continue to be after death before gradually processing the experience and returning to full self-awareness.

Those who remain earthbound were extremely attached to the physical plane when they were incarnate. Rather than passing on to the astral plane, they are stuck in the etheric upper physical plane as ghosts. They did not see beyond earthly pleasures and pain. Those who were addicted to cigarettes, drugs, food, or alcohol are sometimes earthbound because they still crave them mentally and emotionally. They have the opportunity to let go of their addictions any time, although it is easier while one is still physical.

RELATING TO THE INCARNATE

After people die, do they maintain a connection with loved ones left behind?

Generally they do. Sometimes it is necessary to get some perspective on their experiences before they make themselves available to loved ones. Otherwise, they tend to look in on them from time to time, especially in the first several years following death. As time goes on, their attention becomes increasingly focused on the astral plane, unless of course they reincarnate. You can assume that if someone close to you dies, he is staying in touch with you as long as you feel a connection with him; usually it is a mutual thing. If you agree on an essence level to move on, you will not tend to think of each other as much. If one of you stubbornly refuses to let the other go, it can be a hindrance to you both.

If a parent has died while a child is young, she will tend to keep an especially strong connection with the child until he has come of age. You do not forfeit responsibility for those you bring into the world just because you die. A parent will provide a mothering or fathering influence to the child as well as s/he is able to, and may assist the child's spirit guides.

BETWEEN LIFETIMES

How long do people usually spend on the astral plane between incarnations?

It is individual. Some souls feel uncomfortable there and cannot wait to get back into a body, taking the first one that becomes available. Others may feel complete with the cycle of lives they have done and take vacations that could translate into thousands of years on the physical plane. However, fifty to eighty years is typical. It partly depends on the world's current population and therefore the number of available bodies. In times of high population such as today, souls may incarnate into several bodies concurrently.

Some souls, especially those who are almost finished with the physical plane, are choosy about who their parents will be, what kind of body they will have, etc., so it can take a while to find what they are looking for. It is rather like coming near the end of a treasure hunt and needing only certain items.

It seems that on the astral plane, we have a larger awareness and basically know all the lessons we're coming down here to learn. What's the point? Someone capable of torturing and killing on the physical plane has access to larger knowledge and love between lives. Why is it important to come within these constraints to learn the lessons if we already know them?

A person who commits torture and murder may or may not repent on the astral plane, just as he may or may not repent later in his life on the physical plane. Not all souls are the same. The soul is not perfect, all-knowing, or necessarily wise. However, the soul is the larger self and has relatively more understanding than the specific personality on the physical plane. The personality tends to be preoccupied with the physical plane, so the influence of *maya*, or illusion, is stronger.

The soul may be intellectually aware that murder is wrong. However, because of a lack of practical understanding and development, it may not be able to live with the stresses and illusions of the physical plane when incarnate without resorting to it. Even on the physical plane, there are things that people "know" they should not do but they do them anyway; they have not yet experienced true knowing.

An advantage of the astral interval for reviewing your life is potentially greater neutrality. When you do not have a body, your survival is not being threatened. You also have the advantage of seeing that you are part of a larger picture than you realized when you were incarnate. You have greater access to knowledge, such as knowledge of what your life task was. If you killed someone, you can see whether you were paying back karma, creating karma, or neither. You can see what your motivations were and decide what you are going to do in the next lifetime if there needs to be a balancing experience. There are other souls who are available to help in this evaluation process.

Not every soul takes advantage of this perspective, although the laws of karma operate whether or not there is recognition. The acceptance of clarity, like all things, is a matter of choice. Many apparently waste their time during the astral interval just as they waste it when they are on the physical plane, although ultimately, no experience is wasted.

Any time you are embroiled in a situation in which you have no perspective and then get away from it for a while, detaching and reflecting, many things can become clear to you. This is true whether you are physical or astral. People could benefit from much more detached review of their lives while they are in them. There would then be a lot less of it to do during the astral interval. Many live their lives as if they were sleepwalking. There is little review, so most of it must happen astrally. Someone who has stayed up to date while on the physical plane does not need much review when she gets to the astral plane. She can quickly move on to her next step.

TIMES OF DEATH AND BIRTH

Hermetic astrology states that the situation at birth is the same as or the complement of what is present at the death of the previous incarnation. Is this true for all of us, or is this valid only in a few circumstances?

Each lifetime, to some degree, is a continuation of the previous one. Therefore, the astrological configuration of the previous death may be taken into account. When the next lifetime has a different theme, the time of the previous death may not be important.

11 ❧ KARMA

WHAT IS KARMA?

Karma is formed when you significantly violate another's domain, creating an energy imbalance that then seeks resolution. Usually a karmic debt is repaid in kind. For example, if A murders B, B will murder A or A will save the life of B in a subsequent lifetime.

Philanthropic or "good" karma results from significantly expanding another's choices in a way that does not benefit you other than through the good feelings that arise.

WAKING UP

Karma is one way you learn on the physical plane. In karma, you have an extreme experience, and balance it with the opposite extreme experience. By learning both sides of an issue, you can come to a new understanding that puts you consciously in the middle. You may go from one extreme to another, back and forth, for several lifetimes before you finally wake up and find that balanced place.

Suppose that in one lifetime you are murdered and desire revenge, so in the next lifetime you murder the one who murdered you, who now desires revenge. In the lifetime after that one, you become the victim again, and so on. You flip-flop in that way until you wake up and see that you are both the murderer and the murdered. You recognize that both are parts of you, and make peace between them. Then you no longer need to repeat the pattern. That is integration.

CHOICE

You can choose how and when you repay karmic debts. Suppose that you had a lifetime in which you killed people indiscriminately and caused a great deal of suffering. You may start repaying those debts during your next lifetime by having a painful or early death, or suffering great losses. On the other hand, you may decide that for the maximum growth, it would be better to have an experience of what it is like to be really loved. In that case, the next life may be relatively easy and comfortable, perhaps preparing you to repay your debts in a more positive way. You must eventually deal with your karma, and it weighs upon you until you repay it, but sometimes that is put off for centuries or even millennia. That is not usual, though.

Karma is a compelling influence, and if you do not plan how you will repay your debts, you will eventually repay them anyway, but haphazardly. If you are in the vicinity of someone with whom you have a karmic tie, you tend to attract one another. Whether or not you had intended to, once you start the wheels of repayment in motion, it is difficult to stop them. However, although a karmic repayment may appear haphazard, you may actually have chosen it even though you do not consciously remember having done so.

JESUS'S DEATH

Did Jesus's death wipe out accumulated mass karma?

No. Karma, as we define it, is incurred individually. You have to repay your own karma.

So there's no such thing as mass karma?

There is only mass karma in the sense that many individuals may have incurred karma together and may repay it together as well.

VOODOO

Just as someone can literally stick a knife in another person, he can also stick a vibrational knife in him through the intense projection of hate or another destructive force. It is karmic in either case if it significantly harms the other person.

MIND FUCK

If, through manipulation, someone produces deep confusion or disturbance in another person who is not capable of defending himself from it, he has deprived him of choice and therefore has created karma. This could be called *mind fuck*. If you chose parents who ended up planting some negative belief systems in you, welcome to the human race—that is not mind fuck. You chose your parents and got their belief systems. Parents can mind fuck their children, but it would have to be a deliberate and serious infraction.

BEING TRIGGERED

When you are around someone with whom you have strong karmic ties, you can be pulled into a whirlwind of emotion and other forces that you do not understand. You can feel blind because the intensity of what originally created that karma is triggered in you. The more you maintain an objective, neutral consciousness, the better you are able to handle these forces when they come into your life.

GRACE

Grace is the neutralization of karma solely in consciousness, learning its lessons without physically acting it out. Grace is always possible, theoretically, but most pay back their karma physically because they are not yet capable of balancing karma purely in consciousness.

Suppose that a person murders someone in cold blood. He is not likely to seek grace. The fact that he committed this act indicates that he is deeply enmeshed in the karmic state and probably has little vision beyond it. However, for the sake of argument, let's say that after that lifetime, he seeks grace; he does not want to be killed by the person he murdered in a future lifetime. He would have to undergo an enormous amount of growth to receive grace. He would have to develop sufficient empathy and compassion to feel what it was like for the other person. Mere remorse is not enough. Realistically, he is probably going to need to be killed by him and perhaps undergo other physical plane experiences to awaken in that area and learn the lesson. Grasping it without tangible experience may just be too difficult for him.

Grace is more possible when karma is less extreme and its lessons are within easier reach. Grace is not undertaken unilaterally—the victim's soul must agree to it as well. However, since being repaid a karmic debt can be almost as unpleasant as the karma itself, this is usually not a problem. Although grace is usually achieved from the astral plane after the lifetime is complete, it can also be accomplished from the physical plane when the person who created the karma experiences major growth.

Between the two extremes of repaying a karmic debt through "an eye for an eye" and neutralizing it through grace is what might be called *modified grace*. Continuing the example above, modified grace might entail the murderer saving the life of his former victim in a future lifetime, perhaps in a doctor/patient relationship in which the doctor received no pay. This is a more enlightened and compassionate way to repay that karma.

Some karmas can also be worked off from the astral plane, again by the agreement of both parties. Since karma is fundamentally an imbalance of energy, repaying it is a matter of doing whatever it takes to rebalance it. Occasionally, an essence who is otherwise complete with the physical plane attempts to work off a remaining karmic debt from the astral plane rather than reincarnating. If he is not successful, he will need to reincarnate in order to repay the debt.

Part III

THE COLLECTIVE

12 ❧ GOD

UNIVERSAL CONSCIOUSNESS

Every part of the whole has consciousness. The consciousness of one of your fingers is not as large and complex as that of your entire body. Your consciousness is not as large and complex as that of the solar system, which is, in turn, not as large and complex as that of the universe. The consciousness of the universe is sometimes referred to as God. Since you are part of the universe, you are part of God, although the universe has a consciousness beyond the sum of its parts.

If you experience unification among your internal parts, you have a sense of connection with the larger whole that teaches you more about God than twenty philosophy books.

DEFINING GOD

Is there a God?

It depends on how you define this term. [*Thunder was heard at this moment.*] Thank you! You see, "He" does not like being defined! But if you perceive this word to represent the creative force of the universe, or the organizing principle of reality, or the consciousness of the whole, then yes, God exists. In saying that you love God, you are therefore saying that you feel yourself to be part of what is real, what orders and binds things together. However, if you define this term as an Old Testament patriarch who is wrathful when you cross him, then no, no such thing exists. We prefer the term *the Tao* because it brings up fewer preconceptions, although the Tao could be differentiated from God. The Tao could refer to the undimensional source from which universes spring. God would then refer to the highest or overall consciousness of our manifest universe.

THE WAY

The Chinese word "Tao" means "the Way." Why don't you just call it that?

"The Way" sounds a little bit like there is only one way or path. In fact, all life is the Way.

THE EVER-CHANGING GOD

Religion fosters the idea of an unchanging God. God is both unchanging and ever-changing. God does not have to be static to be wise. God flows, and if you are going to be aligned with God, you need to flow, too. You can find stability and comfort in change.

IDENTITY IN GOD

The individual cells of your body each have their own consciousness. All those cells together make up your body. Your body as a whole, however, has a consciousness that responds to the consciousness of all the cells in it but is also something more than just their sum. It acts upon them, bringing something new to them, just as they act upon the overall consciousness. What is commonly thought of as God is similar in its relationship with its parts. God includes everything, yet is more than everything.

A cell in your finger has its own sense of itself, but you could say that it also has larger identities. For example, it is part of your finger, your arm, your entire physical body, and you. Likewise, the totality of God is much greater and wider than what you individually experience, but God is your ultimate identity. Your way of experiencing earth is like nobody else's, so you bring a unique perspective to God.

God is evolving; it is continually learning, at levels we are not capable of comprehending. It does not have all the answers to begin with. Otherwise, why would it go to all the trouble of experiencing the universe? We are all part of God, present in this realm to have experiences. It is a vast and grand affair, with tremendous design and order, yet with great spontaneity and surprise as well. You might say that it is partly about aspects of God discovering or increasing their awareness that they are God and using their power as God to create.

Possibilities are God's playthings. The universe is made up of infinite possibilities, so God will never run out of playthings. God likes to see "what would happen if...." God as a whole does not know until it tries, just like any of us individually. God includes all the knowledge that exists, but there is an infinite amount of knowledge that has not yet been created. Creating knowledge is part of your purpose.

Your connection with God as a whole occurs through your essence, or higher self, which in turn is connected without obstruction to every level of the greater whole. When a person prays, her essence broadcasts her need into the relevant levels, most often to her team of guides on the astral plane but further afield if that would be helpful, and brings back the answer to the extent she is open and able to receive it.

13 ❧ RELIGION

WHAT RINGS TRUE

In all major religions, the original teachings have become distorted with misconceptions to some extent. Part of the reason is that with the passage of time, cultural thinking and lifestyles change, and words take on different meanings. You can observe how much change there has been in this regard since Shakespeare's time. If Shakespeare were the founder of a religion rather than a playwright, and if people were hanging on his every word, interpreting them in terms of present-day understanding, some quite bizarre ideas could develop. People look too much to externals for guidance. Even if the externals are apparently the words of a great teacher, truth is alive and must be experienced as a living thing to be known.

You have to decide for yourself what rings true. If it is true, it should have some logic to it. However, everyone is entitled to his own beliefs. Those on higher planes don't always agree, either.

UPLIFTING THE BODY

You have said that because we are in primate bodies, our civilization tends to revolve around primate tribal ideas. That sometimes results in behavior I find to be crude and infantile, especially in relationships.

Being sentient brings what is present in the life form to higher and higher levels of realization. Its characteristics before sentience are the raw materials. The human body's primate tendencies are not wrong but they can manifest in crude, less appropriate ways. The more experienced the essence, the less it identifies with the body and the more it recognizes the body's possibilities of higher function.

This process of uplifting the experience of the body

happens with each individual over a series of lifetimes. It can also be seen in microcosm within a single lifetime—as you mature, you tend to be better able to harness the body's drives rather than being controlled by them. The process occurs collectively as well, so that over time, the civilization, and ultimately the species itself, is elevated and develops expanded capabilities.

This process might be called transcending the body, but that idea is usually misunderstood. It is thought that as people become more civilized, they must deny the impulses of the body and become more separate from the body's urges. Many religionists decry the lust of the body, for example. This is an incorrect interpretation of the process of ascension. Its purpose is to bring the body to a new level of experience, not to squash its impulses.

PRAYER

I pray every morning for guidance or success, but it seems that I'm praying to a blank wall.

There is nothing wrong with asking for assistance, both from other people and from God (or from spirit guides and other nonphysical beings). Nonetheless, you have primary responsibility for creating what you pray for. It is said that God helps those who help themselves. Helping yourself is not simply a matter of your doing more materially but of opening to your spiritual power as part of the whole. By spiritual power we do not mean some disembodied or ethereal energy, or a religious technique—we mean your presence. When some people walk into a room, you can feel their presence. Your presence gives you the ability to create. True prayer is not like a child asking her father to give something such as a raise in allowance or a new doll. It is stating your acceptance of what you are asking for. For example, if you pray for good health, you are really saying,

"I'm willing to be healthy and to do what is necessary to be healthy. I tune in to and receive from the health-promoting forces of the universe." It is primarily your own presence that draws it to you.

RELIGIONS AND THE NEW AGE

There is value in diversity. Many people are not attracted to the New Age movement, and it would not necessarily serve everyone's growth well. We do not foresee one universal religion or belief system on earth for some time. It is not practical when people are coming from such different places. You cannot necessarily expect others to understand your viewpoints and accept your right to them, but you can work toward understanding those of others and accepting their right to them. If you live with integrity and grace, there will likely be people who are interested in knowing how you view life.

STRUCTURE

The world's religions offer structures to hang on to for those who otherwise might feel adrift in a senseless world. They give an awareness that there is order in the universe and meaning behind events. In the absence of direct knowledge, this can be valuable, even when the teachings are not themselves that valid or useful.

LIVING SYMBOLS

It is easier to move gradually from the old to the new than to throw away the old and have nothing on which to build in creating the new. The new can look less frightening with a foundation of what was wise and good in the old. This partly explains the resurgence of interest in ancient traditions. Traditions and rituals impede growth when those participating in them have rigid ideas about what they mean. For them, they are no longer living symbols, and people often just go through the motions. However, if you retrieve old rituals about which you have no jaded views, you can recycle them and have new experiences.

On the other hand, all traditions and rituals were invented somewhere along the way. You should not hesitate to invent new ones as the need arises.

14 ❧ INDIVIDUAL AND COLLECTIVE CONSCIOUSNESS

THOUGHT

Pure thought is not created by consciousness. Thought exists as a potential reality. Consciousness draws from the infinite well of potential thought that is available and collects it around itself.

Your brain is a highly sophisticated biocomputer. It is used by your consciousness as a means of manifesting thought. When an essence is incarnate, it brings part of its consciousness into the biocomputer, which processes and stores it. All sentient (self-aware, choice-making) creatures, whether or not they have brains, have a means of processing and storing part of their essence's consciousness.

Individual consciousness joins into collective consciousness. For instance, there is the collective consciousness of all human beings on earth. There is the collective consciousness of this entire universe—all consciousness in it is part of it. It gives rise to what is known as God.

KNOWLEDGE

Does intelligence grow from life to life as you learn things?

Intelligence as it is usually thought of is largely a function of heredity and imprinting. However, talents and knowledge grow with experience. For example, let's say you were an accomplished musician in a past life. In this lifetime, you don't play a musical instrument and you are not involved in music, but you develop your spiritual perception. The next lifetime in which you play a musical instrument, you will not only carry forward the substance of what you previously learned about music but you also may be able to play music with the added spiritual perception developed in the present lifetime, which would add a dimension to your playing. It all fits together.

THOUGHT CREATES

[*Question asked at a lecture.*] *If we create all things with our thoughts, are you a creation of our group mind?*

Although all things spring from thought, obviously no one individual or group creates all things. However, it is up to you to validate for yourself if we, the Michael entity, are a creation of the group mind of those present. Let us know what you decide!

CHOOSING A TOPIC

[*Question asked at a lecture.*] *With so many truths to speak about, why did you choose to speak on these particular ones to this group?*

These topics are apropos for many right now in view of larger influences at work. How many of you find them to be relevant to your life this week? [*Most present raised their hands.*] Most of you do not know one another, so you have not been discussing these subjects. We are all one, and certain subjects are issues for the collective mind at specific times. Had we been giving this talk somewhere else at this time, it might have been similar, although the specific wording is dictated by its appropriateness for those present. We wish to speak in a way that you can receive.

15 ❧ GROUP ENERGY

MULTIPLICATION OF OPENNESS

The whole is greater than the sum of its parts. This is why many consider marriage sacred—people know on some level that two can be greater than one plus one. A human being with thirty-seven trillion cells is capable of more than what thirty-seven trillion single-celled organisms are capable of. When a group is open to energies from other dimensions of reality through a channel, there is a multiplication of the individual openness.

BLENDING IN A GROUP

There is much satisfaction available from participating in a group consciousness that is light-centered. The physical plane tends to emphasize individual experience. Group awareness is usually limited to perhaps church on Sunday, political groupings, and maybe even mobs that have a chaotic or destructive intent. Individual experience is valid and necessary. You must understand who you are before you can properly blend in a group. However, there is much value and reward if one is capable of coming into a group on the right basis.

An experience of group is different from that of individuality or partnership. The transition from being a collection of individuals who are near others to truly being a group can be achieved with no loss of individuality. We speak to you as a group, 1,050 essences working for common purposes, yet each essence is individual. Paradoxically, the greater our experience of oneness, the more our individuality is enhanced, although our focus tends to be at the group level. We did not come together in this intimate way until we had each completed a cycle of lifetimes as individuals on the physical plane. We would not have been ready for such closeness.

If there is deep blending in a group meditating, the energy that moves out can be profoundly influential. Each person can contribute to the development of collective energy by taking responsibility for letting the highest possible vibration be established. Being clear about the greater purpose for which the group has assembled, being sensitive to the whole, letting go of individual concerns, and deliberately allowing bonding to occur are also helpful.

People who gather in throngs may be effective when a leader is present. However, if the participants are not taking responsibility for the group experience, it generally falls apart when the leader is gone. Responsibility is often avoided at all costs, but this word in its highest sense indicates an ability to function effectively in creating experience. Why would people not wish to be responsible? When it is truly seen, it is not avoided. Of course, a child is less capable of responsibility than an adult. A child might be able to be responsible for his toys but not for running a household. So there are varying levels of responsibility that one can take. At whatever level you are, you can take responsibility. The alternative is to be a victim.

I work a lot in bars doing music, and I notice that the people seem willing to blend their energies. Is alcohol helpful?

Generally not. Alcohol does loosen restraint so that blending is easier, but it also decreases the quality. The finer the perceptions, the higher the quality of blending available.

I have a problem connecting with what's going on now in the group. I tend to drift in and out. Why is this?

In a group in which part of the intent is to open awareness on higher levels, the levels where you usually know yourself have to adjust. It is like a bodybuilder being given a weight heavier than he is accustomed to; he may stagger around a little as he adjusts to it. He can handle it but he needs to get his bearings. Eventually, you will adjust to these higher levels of awareness so that you can maintain them simultaneously with your usual conscious awareness.

TRANSFORMING UNHEALTHY ATMOSPHERES

If you are aware of group energy, you can have a greater experience of it, and if it is not healthy, you can be a force of change in it.

Suppose that you attend a meeting at which the group energy leaves something to be desired. Perhaps many people are out of sorts and the group energy reflects it. You could ask within that the energy be altered through you with the help of your guides, essence, and other people attending who, at least unconsciously, share your desire to improve it. As you open to let the energy move through you, you at first might feel greater discomfort. It is like being an air filter pulling in pollution. However, as you let it flow, the discomfort passes, and you feel the fresh air coming out through you.

Your impact will vary, based on what you are working with. There may be times when the atmosphere is so polluted that you cannot significantly alter it. When that is the case, you might want to seal your own atmosphere. How is this done? Mainly by asking for it. You can also visualize a bubble around you keeping in pure, clean "air" and keeping out pollution. Don't resist the pollution but simply choose to vibrate at a different quality.

Whether or not you are consciously seeking to improve the atmosphere you are in, your presence is a positive influence when you carry a loving intent.

16 ❧ INTENT

The formation of group consciousness involves the establishment of a connection from each individual to a central idea. The more people who funnel their individuality into an idea at the same time, the more of that idea there is to share. If the idea (or the person or place representing the idea) is capable of accepting the interest that is brought individually, the interest is joined, and its contributors begin to feel joined to one another, not because of lateral association, but because of interest in this central idea.

A powerful and energizing process of great multiplication occurs when a common idea is adhered to, for either constructive or destructive ends. Destructive ideas contain the seeds of self-destruction that must eventually manifest. Likewise, ideas with a loving intent inevitably bring benefit to those who hold them. This may not be observed immediately, but it will be.

Most people go to work or spend their days doing something that involves others. As an example of intent, let's look at a company that makes cars. The intent of those who own and run the company is presumably that the company make money through manufacturing good cars. However, let's say that most of the employees have a different intent: to collect their paycheck and not be too miserable while they do so. They are not aligned with the intent of this whole, so there is not a multiplication of power. The main reason Japanese car manufacturers became more productive than those in the U.S. is the greater experience of aligned intent: Japanese workers shared management's intent that their company make money through manufacturing good cars. Good management techniques encourage aligned intent, and aligned intent leads to better management techniques. However, aligned intent is primarily responsible for their greater productivity, not management techniques alone.

If aligned intent brings a multiplication of power, what

would happen if added to their intent was the intent to bring peace on earth? The intent would then be to bring peace through making money manufacturing good cars. "Oh, but we don't have time to think about peace," might be the reply. However, bringing peace does not necessarily require additional time spent. The real reason that peace—we are just using this as an example—is not part of the intent of such a company is that those involved do not particularly want peace. They might say, "Of course we want peace. Everyone wants peace." However, it is evidently not a high priority. If it were, there would be substantial energy invested in it.

The company's priorities of intent are probably profit, cars through which to make profit, and whatever is necessary to make cars with which to make profit, in that order. Workers who are completely aligned with the company would have the same priorities. The highest priorities of other workers might include such things as money, job security, family, vacations, and relationships. None of these priorities is wrong—it is for each person to decide. However, choices are made by both commission and omission. Peace may not be the highest priority simply because it is not deliberately chosen to be, for whatever reason. Many people do not believe that they have the power to help create peace, so they do not even consider the possibility.

Those for whom peace has highest priority tend to have peace, just as those for whom money is the highest priority tend to have money. Sometimes there is a gap between what you think you want and what you have. This is especially true if you have only decided relatively recently what you want and you are still in the process of manifesting it. However, often what you think you want is not what you really want. If you wish to know what you really want, look at the choices you are actually making. If you are speaking a good deal about what you think you want but are not doing very much about it, your priority clearly is to talk about what you think you want. This is not wrong either—maybe you are just getting used to the idea of what you might want and you are not ready to have it yet. However, if that is the case, you will save energy if you do not worry about why you have not yet created what you say you want.

Maybe what you really want most right now is to do nothing. That may be your highest good, eventually leading to more productivity than if you forced yourself to do what is on your mental agenda. If you are choosing to do nothing, you will enjoy it much more if you acknowledge that choice and fully get into doing nothing. If your avowed intent is in conflict with your experience, you are burdened with a split focus—you are not fully doing nothing, yet you are not doing the thing you think you should do. If you do nothing with all your heart, you might do it beautifully and effectively for two days rather than doing nothing halfheartedly for two months. That might so satisfy your need for nothing that you will be through with it and ready to move on to the next thing. It is wise to choose what you really want and to live fully in your choices. If you are not satisfied with them, change them—choices may be altered at any time. Be quick to do so if they are not working for you.

Do not criticize yourself for your past choices. In a sense, you cannot make a wrong choice. There is value in every choice you ever made, partly because it gave you practice in making choices. If you are harboring guilt or misgivings about choices you made in the past, think about what each choice taught you about choice-making. You will be surprised at how quickly you are able to let go of your discomfort about past choices.

Why would a person want to do nothing?

Rest is the usual reason. A person may also need to go within and handle some issues that have been hanging around unfinished for a long time. Sometimes a person does this by being sick because freedom from outer activity permits this.

Even if he is not consciously thinking about those issues, he may be reflecting on them at other levels. You are not necessarily free to do this when you are active.

Individuality and group consciousness is a duality in need of healing and uniting, like male and female, and light and dark. It is usually thought that one excludes the other. Americans tend to fear that they will lose their individuality if they work effectively in a group. The Japanese tend to fear that unless there is conformity to the group, society will break down. However, individuality is known most when it is combined with effective function within larger groups. American individuality has created ideas and inventions that have spurred the world, but sometimes they have been more fully realized by countries with more effective group functioning. Individual and collective effectiveness can coexist in the same people.

The Japanese recognize the value of individual contributions to a limited extent: if someone on an assembly line contributes an idea for making that assembly line better, that is usually acceptable. Ironically, in the U.S. where individuality is so prized, such individual contributions have not been as welcomed. Perhaps it is because those in charge want to do things their way. They sacrifice the individuality of others for their own, because they do not adequately value the good of the group. When the individual and the group are in balance, there is both maximum individual and group effectiveness.

Just as some people are more male-energied and some are more female-energied, the United States emphasizes the individual more, and Japan, the group. It is not that Americans need to lose individuality to function better in groups. They simply need more respect for the ways in which proper group function can enhance individuality, just as the Japanese need more respect for the ways in which appropriate individuality can enhance group function. It is similar to men needing to have great respect for and sensitivity to female energy if male energy is going to have its fulfillment, and vice versa for women.

To give another example: if you wish to write a book individually, you may still need a publisher, editor, illustrator, booksellers, and so forth. If you work with a good editor, your writing may improve—more of your individuality may come out. The other collaborators can help you reach your audience.

When we express our individuality, we resonate with others' individuality, making us one. Individuality actually creates the group.

Yes, and the more you experience your individuality, the more you foster that in others, allowing you and others to share an effective group experience. As in all true polarities, the two elements depend on one another.

Those truly manifesting their individuality (as opposed to ego) tend to respect the individuality of others, promoting cooperation and unity. For example, when the director, actors, cinematographer, designers, and everyone else participating in making a film are at their most creative, they tend to respect the creativity of their collaborators, allowing the best possible film to result.

I would like to feel that everything I do promotes peace on earth, but my consciousness of that gets lost in my immediate goals.

If you wish to have more intent about peace, either world or local, think about it more. Notice ways you could promote it, just as you would notice ways you could make more money if money were your intent. To give an example, you might ask that your meditations contribute to world peace. Like the car manufacturers who can create peace while making cars, you can create peace while doing whatever else you do during your meditation. It is not like your Christmas list for Santa in which you can have either a dollhouse or a bicycle. You can have whatever you ask for; you just have to be willing to accept the consequences of having requested it. It could change your life to ask that your function enhance world peace. If you are willing for your life to be changed, then ask.

If you choose to create world peace, you increasingly live in a peaceful world. You become peaceful about problems rather than charged and agitated. You are not oblivious to those whose lives are not peaceful, but for you they are a part of your peaceful world. You are compassionate toward those who are making unpeaceful choices, and because of this, you have more to offer those who want peace to some degree but have not yet chosen it.

When you meditate and genuinely ask for something such as peace or light, it generally comes quickly. That may cause you to wonder why you did not ask for it before. Few people actually ask for peace. "Ask and it shall be given." Asking is opening to receive. If you value peace, ask for it.

The main reason people tend not to value peace is that they are enmeshed in their battles, inner and outer. They think that they have to wait for resolution in order to be peaceful. However, if they let go to peace first, they would more easily resolve their battles.

When you are fully with your choices, they complete their cycle more quickly. When people choose violence fully rather than being lukewarm, it reaches its fulfillment, one way or another, just as peace does when it is fully chosen. Those who choose peace are magnetized toward it and tend to be out of the way of violence.

In choosing peace, you are not trying to change those who have chosen violence. You are offering choice to those who have not yet chosen, those who have an openness to peace. There are those who are drawn to peace and those who are drawn to violence. Those who feel the compulsion toward peace, even if their current experience is not peaceful, will move in the direction of peace. You can support them in their movement.

Your intent is powerful. The more you use it consciously, the more power you experience in your life. Although not choosing is a choice and a powerful one, it is a choice that can create confusion—powerful confusion sometimes. The more you know that you are choosing constantly—what to eat, what to wear, where to go—the more you can use those choices as points of power to achieve what you really want. Every word you say is your choice. Words can be atom bombs or gifts of love. They can be laser beams of creative action or careless graffiti sprayed on others' walls. It is powerful to choose consciously whether to speak or be silent, as well as what to say and how to say it, if you do speak.

Again, any choice is a good choice, in a sense, because it leads to results, and results teach you. If you do not like the results in your life, learn from them and make other choices.

17 ❧ PERFORMING AND ENERGY

Performing allows energy to move through what is being performed to the audience. Many accomplished performers learn to work with larger amounts of energy than they normally would if they were not performers. They give and receive it with hundreds or thousands of audience members. If the performer is fairly unblocked, it passes through like water through a faucet, not hurting the faucet. It is felt while it is moving through.

Those who are self-destructive or do not learn how to get out of the way of energy movement can burn out. Incidentally, people who quickly dissipate large sums of money also usually lack the ability to handle substantial energy.

You may have noticed that good performers seem more substantial or larger somehow. All energy ultimately is love. Those who handle energy best are those who, at least in some respects, are loving. Successful performers often have something loving about them. In some cases, the public persona is loving and the private one, which has not caught up to the public persona, is less loving. A condition not unlike schizophrenia results. The most complete performers are those in whom the public and private personas are blended, and in whom both are loving.

It is not to be expected that many performers will be capable of a consistent loving attitude in all aspects of their lives. There will be gaps, as there are for virtually all people. Those who perform, though, will feel more pressure on their gaps because they are handling larger quantities of energy than most. This holds true for others in the public eye, such as preachers, politicians, newscasters, and writers. Even novelists who avoid public exposure personally attract large amounts of energy.

Let's differentiate here between quantity and quality of energy. Usually those in the public eye attract a large quantity of relatively low-quality energy. High-quality energy is sometimes called healing energy. It is light-filled and fine in texture rather than coarse. Performers can help raise the quality of energy. If, while performing, coarse energy comes through you, you can send it back to the audience a little bit more refined, and people will feel uplifted. They may interpret it as liking your performance, and that may, of course, be the case. However, there are many aspects of performance, both seen and unseen. The energetic aspect is primary—all invisible influences are actually primary in life.

Energy can be focused or unfocused. When it is focused, something is achieved. In performance, the goal is to focus energy so it can move creatively. An audience before a performance is completely unfocused. People are chitchatting amongst themselves, and the energy is chaotic. There is plenty of energy, but it is not doing anything. Think of the enormous amounts of energy in the New York subway system during rush hour. It is not changing the world, for either better or worse, because it is not focused.

Of course, all energy does not need to be focused, but a time of performance is rather like a time of worship, a drawing together of energies to raise them. If you perform for an audience whose members are eating, drinking, or talking, you may notice that less focusing of energy occurs, and it is less satisfying for that reason.

When you perform alone, you are the only one who needs to be focused to begin with. When you perform with a group, the group must be focused among itself. The more focus there is, the more energy can move in a single direction, and the more will be felt by all involved. The quality of your working relationship directly affects the focus. Part of this working relationship is morale, mutual support, and sensitivity to the others in the group, and part of it is technical proficiency. In general, the better the group's functioning, the more fun and satisfaction everyone will have, because more energy will move and it will be of a higher quality.

When an audience and a performer align or "click," there can be magic, an upliftment or even healing that is often beyond the comprehension of most participating. It is not seen and only its exterior part is felt, yet it speaks to something deep in all. The healing may be more on the emotional level, in which case an outpouring of emotion may be experienced. It may be more on the intellectual level, resulting in a greater clarity and knowledge of truth. Or it may be more on an energetic level—people may feel lightheaded or even high. People can have a "spiritual experience" during any kind of performance, although they would not necessarily identify it as one, and the quality of the experience depends on the quality of the consciousness shared.

When you are dealing with large amounts of energy, you draw spirit guides whose function is to help manage it. Letting go is important because it permits your guides to do their job, just as your job may be to sing.

Sometimes gifted performers who have an innate ability to work with energy let it go to their heads. They think that they are doing this marvelous thing all by themselves. They are only helping organize the energies of all present. When there is a transcendent experience, you can be sure that there is participation in it from higher levels of being.

Part IV

CHANGING THE WORLD

18 ~ IMAGINATION

You are vast. This vastness has been achieved over eons. It is no small thing, even though you may take it for granted. The vaster a consciousness, the greater its imagination, in the sense that it can conceive of more. In your consciousness, you can take the form of anything of which you are aware. You could imagine yourself taking the form of a snake, although a snake could not imagine itself taking the form of a human. You might say that imagination is not real, yet what you imagine is real on a certain level. Inventors imagine that something that does not exist in form actually does, and then proceed to bring it into form. The larger the imagination, the greater the expansion of imagination that can occur. In other words, imagination begets still greater imagination.

Can you imagine a world that is loving and peaceful? Many people cannot. If you can, you can work to make that imagining increasingly specific. What would a loving and peaceful world be like? This is no different from Edison imagining what a phonograph might be like. He had to have a specific idea about it; otherwise he would not have been able to invent it.

Those with the greatest imaginations ultimately have the most impact. Visionary artists not recognized in their day may eventually be celebrated for their imagination—people were not able to recognize it at the time but eventually they did as their own capacity expanded. The act of imagining can push aside other people's limitations.

If you have a vision of yourself as being small and worthless, yet someone else is wise enough to hold a vision of you as being large and worthy, eventually his vision will likely have an impact on you if you let it. If someone has believed in you when you have not believed in yourself, you know how powerful that can be. How much better it is to imagine yourself as being what you want to be without waiting for someone else to do it. If you hold to this vision, in time it will likely manifest.

The world is deeply in need of role models. No one is quite sure anymore whom they want to emulate. Everyone's shortcomings are amplified under the scrutiny of the media. Many heroes of days gone by would not look so wonderful under such scrutiny. In the absence of external role models, the ability to imagine is especially vital: if you can imagine yourself to be vast and great, your innate vastness and greatness can begin to manifest, although perhaps in different ways than you thought it would. You can revise the specifics of your image as you go along and learn more about it, just as Edison did while inventing.

The universe is an act of imagination on the part of the Tao. Each person is a microcosm of the Tao, creating a universe in imagination. Imagine that you live in a world of peace, love, and prosperity for all, or at least imagine that this is possible. We are not suggesting that you blind yourself to the present situation, but spend time seeing alternatives. Put your vision into practice in whatever ways you can. Hold to it.

At first, your vision may spread only as a vision: others may, by the sheer force of your vision, also imagine that something different is possible. They may share the details of their vision with you, increasing yours. When enough people share the vision, it may begin to manifest. This can occur much faster than you might think. An example of this is political changes occurring that might have been thought impossible not long ago.

Your image of a peaceful, loving world is less effective if it is merely philosophy. If you work with it, it will guide you to generate peace and love in your own life. Like refining a blueprint of a house as you build it, you may refine your vision. You might discover, for example, that peace does not require everyone to agree, and that love is not always soft. In discovering the true nature of your vision, your imagining becomes more specific and therefore more effective. Your growth leads to the growth of your vision, and finally to the growth of the whole, because you influence the whole.

19 ❧ CONTINUAL EVOLUTION

Your growth as an individual, although it is your responsibility, does not happen in a vacuum. You could not have the awareness you do outside the context of the whole in which you participate. Not only is each part of the whole evolving, but the whole is evolving as well. Your individual movement cannot be separated from the movement of the whole. Your consciousness down the road will bear little resemblance to what it is now, partly because the consciousness of the whole itself will have progressed.

Since the whole is greater than the sum of its parts, the progression of the whole is more than the evolution of each part within it. Nonetheless, you are an integral part of this process. The whole is obviously made up of its parts. Your achievements contribute to the whole. If you did not individually progress, the whole would not progress as much. Fortunately, although it is possible to slow things down and make them difficult, one cannot halt the process of individual or group evolution.

Some people look back at a point in the past and say, "I was so ignorant then." However, relative to the present, others were as well, if they have been growing. Your awareness then was perfect for that time, and so was everyone else's. Ten years from now, you may look back to today and think that you were in the Dark Ages, and relatively speaking, that would be true. But when does the progression end?

We are all alchemists, you might say, transforming lead into gold. Each person has a world that is leaden to some degree. You are the alchemist in the midst of yours, seeing to what extent you can transform it into gold. Your world may be more leaden than you would like it to be, but you have to start with what you have.

Transformation does not occur overnight. The evolution of worlds is very gradual, but nevertheless certain. Small, incremental movements get the job done.

It is the direct, skillful bringing to bear of the love vibration that is the magic in this alchemy. The more you experience agape—unconditional love—the more you can bring it to bear on your world. That is what will change it. The process is as important and beautiful as the goal itself.

This is an accelerated time—consciousness is growing more rapidly than in the past. However, it is just one step in a process of continual evolution.

20 ❧ RESPONSIBILITY

The future is ever-changing. Every significant decision you make changes your future. Some future events are more easily changed than others. For example, if a person is in the final stages of a terminal illness, it might be difficult to change what would otherwise be inevitable. However, until something actually happens, it is not assured—there is always hope. If things are moving strongly in one direction, it does no good to bury one's head in the sand and pretend that is not the case, but neither does it pay to be a fatalist. Even if death cannot be averted, it can be worthwhile to change the way dying is experienced.

You are the primary creator of your life, but you cannot control everything that happens in it. For one thing, other people are creating *their* lives, and they affect yours to some degree. Lives contain both order and chaos, so although many events spring from your life plan, some are surprises even to your essence—they come out of left field. Losing or finding a job, forming or ending a relationship, and getting sick or well cannot always be foreseen, at least not well in advance.

Those who consciously create their reality are interested in causation, whereas "control freaks" try to control effects and are therefore controlled by them. Usually, this is partly a result of feeling inadequate to handle surprises.

It is the course of wisdom to embrace life's surprises. How much fun would it be to play video games if there were no surprises? If you always knew that Pac-Man would enter the screen from the same place at the same time, you would get good at that game in a hurry and not feel very motivated to keep playing. Life is the greatest game there is. Your being born indicates that you decided to play it. Of course, no one will be delighted if one of his surprises includes his house burning down or some other calamity. But such things, when they do happen, are still part of the game.

Ironically, being overly controlling prevents one from creating the future one wants. By the time you know about something, it is an effect of a previous cause and is moving into the past. Manipulating effects keeps you in the past so that the future you create reflects the past. Only in the now can you change the causes of your future.

You cannot change someone else's future, only your own, and you can only change your future through those choices that are yours to make. However, there is usually much more you can do in any situation than you recognize, and discerning what your choices truly are is extremely valuable. Perhaps part of the reason many want to appropriate other people's choices is that they do not fully recognize their own, like a child wanting other children's toys when he already has a large number. You create your future out of your choices.

Many people do not make a lot of conscious choices. That is their choice. However, if they prefer to drift, holding the attitude that whatever happens will happen, they are stuck with the situations that just happen to come along. What happens to come along will be strongly influenced by the dynamics of their subconscious. They might think that it all originated externally, but that is not the case. A person never stops creating his reality—he creates it either consciously or unconsciously.

People are often passive in living their lives because they do not wish to take responsibility for them. They see other people or "fate" as being responsible—or to blame, if they wish to find fault. It is perhaps the final initiation into spiritual adulthood to take full responsibility for your life. Taking responsibility isn't the same as believing you cause everything that happens to you, although it's useful to explore whatever part your thoughts, feelings, and energies may play in what happens. It simply means that whatever happens, you step up to the plate and handle it, no matter what the cause was. You endeavor to create the best possible future through the choices you make now.

If you were in a car crash, did you create this out of a negative belief? Not necessarily. It *is* possible that the accident was magnetized by something in you such as a death wish or another self-destructive belief, or that you were repaying a karmic debt. It is also possible that you or another driver simply made a random mistake, or that road conditions were bad, such as an unseen ice patch. Perhaps a driver suddenly veered to avoid hitting a dog that no one could foresee would run out into the street. The physical plane has many hazards.

Taking responsibility for the crash doesn't necessarily mean that you claim culpability. If you made a mistake that caused it or at least contributed to it, it is good to acknowledge that. Regardless, taking responsibility means that you make the choices that are now yours to make. You are responsible because you continually have choices to make. No one else is responsible for making your choices. Harry Truman famously said, "The buck stops here." He was not saying, "I caused every problem." He was saying, "I'm willing to do something about it."

When something goes awry, it is assumed that someone must be blamed. Blame is usually charged with hatred so that others can avoid taking responsibility. That does not help matters. The way things come into being is usually complex. Often people oversimplify and categorize because they don't wish to engage with how complicated things are and work to find true solutions. They feel more secure and resolved about fiascos if they can say, "Well, now we know who is to blame." It may be useful to trace the chain of events and see what can be learned and corrected. It may be that one person's choice was particularly pivotal in what happened. Still, there are likely many other factors that need studying. If someone was negligent and broke the law, he would rightly be subject to it and pay whatever penalty is deemed appropriate. However, the most important thing is to solve underlying problems so that the fiasco will not be repeated. This can be better done if no one is demonized, if instead the attitude is taken that we're all in this together.

Punishment, in the sense of deliberately causing suffering to those who transgress, is cruel and serves no practical purpose. The best way to prevent someone who has been stealing, for example, from doing it in the future is to find out why he has been stealing and correct the problem. Perhaps he has been stealing because he is hungry, and if he were taught a skill by which he could earn enough money, he might not steal anymore. Someone else might steal to get attention, and might benefit from therapy. Another person might steal because he is lazy and immoral, and if he has no interest in raising his morality, he might need to be kept separate from society so that society is not under the threat of his stealing. However, this does not imply that he must be caused undue pain. On the contrary, if he is treated with compassion while incarcerated, he might open his heart.

When you blame, you are inflicting pain; when you blame yourself, you are inflicting pain on yourself. When society blames, it is saying, "We collectively do not wish to take responsibility for the way things are." There is a hopeful trend today toward greater societal self-examination, of seeking the underlying causes of problems rather than blaming. Blame is the greatest single cause of war. They say that what goes around, comes around. If you inflict pain on others, no doubt they will try to inflict pain on you before long. Unconscious people tend not to examine their past actions and consider the possibility that others are retaliating. There will not be peace on earth until the desire to inflict pain is replaced with a desire to take responsibility. Until this occurs, there may be a need at times to resort to violence to prevent something even worse, but a compassionate person is saddened, not gleeful, when any harm must be done. Lesser evils such as embargoes may still cause hardship, and they too should be tempered with compassion as much as possible.

If someone else caused an accident that harmed you, you are technically a victim of it. Taking responsibility does not imply that you would never, for example, sue someone if it were warranted, but you would be clear that being the victim of this accident is not your identity. It is just something about which you have choices to make.

A responsible person might sometimes decide that he cannot make choices at the moment, acknowledging perhaps that he doesn't have the energy or can't think clearly. In being clear that you cannot choose right now, you are still acknowledging your responsibility and implying that you will choose later. In the meantime, you might rely on others' help.

If you are injured in an accident, the ways it changes your future depends a great deal on how you approach it. Some people have dramatic recoveries that seemed medically impossible. Others passively slide downhill. You never stop creating your reality. Those with determination who acknowledge their responsibility tend to make the best of it. You may be a victim of particular circumstances, but you are not a victim of life—that is an important distinction.

Some of what you deal with is the result of imbalances you ignorantly created in other lifetimes or earlier in this lifetime. In such a case you might take the attitude that you are a victim of yourself: "I made a dumb mistake and now I have this problem." In a sense, yes, but that is the way it is for everyone. You play the game the best you can—sometimes it looks as if you are winning and sometimes, losing. The fact is that, ultimately, everyone wins this game, *and* everyone makes many mistakes along the way. If you are suffering under the burden of ill health that relates to lifetimes you lived before, that is the way it is, part of the game you are playing. You are responsible but you are not really a victim of yourself. You are a human being doing the best you can, growing as you handle the results of doing the best you can. As you accept whatever you are dealing with and take responsibility for interacting with it in the most intelligent way possible, you heal in the quickest way available to you. You also accumulate much understanding and mastery that you might not have gained otherwise.

Taking responsibility is liberating, and is the only way to win the game. Attempting to stamp out scapegoats never won the game for anyone. You cannot truly love until you take responsibility.

21 ❧ THE ADOLESCENT CIVILIZATION

Love is a much-misunderstood force. Agape, the pure essence of love, is the goal, ultimately, for all. Since it has not been experienced to a great degree, it is easy to see why it has not been understood. People know that it is important. Most popular music, for example, discusses love. Those on a spiritual path often refer to unconditional love.

What is love? Love is like blood circulating in a body, coming from somewhere on its way somewhere else, yet always permeating the entire body. A person with no blocks can experience the free movement of love, bringing a state of contentment and well-being.

Language is inadequate to describe love. In English, you might say that you love your car. It is possible that you are holding unconditional love and it is flowing in that moment toward your automobile. However, how truly you love your car will be demonstrated when you have a flat tire!

Agape is said to be impersonal. Impersonal can mean cold—you might describe a bureaucrat as being impersonal. Personal love sounds much nicer, doesn't it? You would be more likely to associate warmth with personal love than with impersonal love. Someone who gives forth impersonal love and not personal love might seem detached, untouchable, and devoid of drama. In fact, agape is both personal and impersonal. It is impersonal in the sense that it is not restricted to particular persons. In other words, if there is an experience of agape, it may be felt especially keenly as it is reflected back from a particular human being, but it does not exclude any person. In the moment that agape is experienced, an unloving energy cannot at the same time be harbored toward someone else. You can prove this. The next time that you feel wholly loving toward someone, see if you can hate someone else at the same moment. You cannot. You may be aware of some things that need to be clarified between you and another person. However, you could not harbor an attitude of wanting to get even with him, for example. Agape is also personal. It engages with specific persons. Agape encompasses everything, not just human beings, but on the physical plane, other persons give you your greatest opportunity to learn it.

Love is initially a force that emanates from the Tao to empower each universe. In its entry into a universe, you might say that it is shapeless. It is the raw material and motivation for all existence. Every act, in a sense, is an act of love, because existence itself is founded upon this emanation. After love's entry into a universe, it begins to bring forth shapes, rudimentary shapes to begin with, then increasingly complex shapes. These shapes are part of love's thrust to increase the Tao. When you behold the magnificence of nature, you can easily recognize that the shapes of nature are manifestations of love. You can sometimes even see that in other human beings. But often it is a challenge where other people are concerned because of so much that does not appear to embody love.

When children reach adolescence, they often go through awkward changes. In their effort to establish themselves as being separate from their parents, they may experience personality shifts. What was once a sweet child might become a nasty teenager, and what was a cute, well-proportioned body might become ungainly and pimply. Pleasing voices may begin to crack, and so forth. Is love being increased or decreased? For the moment, it looks as if it is being decreased, but in fact, it is being increased. It cannot be seen at this point where all these changes are heading. Some children who go through relatively few changes as teenagers, who are well-behaved and considered to be manageable by their parents and teachers, may as adults contribute relatively little to the world. Others who are quite difficult may make extraordinary contributions later on. In fact, those contributions may be quite significant even during those adolescent years, whether or not the adults involved realize how they are benefiting.

Like individuals, civilizations go through stages of development, and humanity is currently in adolescence. The majority of adolescents do not get into extreme trouble. In the same way, civilizations on most planets with sentient life are not as destructive during their adolescent phase as humans have been. You might say that this civilization has been going through adolescence with a severe case of cracking voices, pimples, and nasty attitudes, with extremes of selfishness and violence. There is special concern at this juncture because this unruly adolescent has many powerful ways to destroy life on the surface of the planet, including itself.

Sometimes parents pray that their children will survive their teenage years, knowing that if they do, they will be all right. Parents also pray that they themselves will survive their teenagers! If humanity survives, if it does not do the equivalent of getting drunk on a Saturday night and smashing a car into a tree, it will grow up and likely be quite a nice young adult, being all the wiser for its rabble-rousing, like the ugly duckling who becomes a beautiful swan. Teenagers can blossom seemingly overnight, and humanity is on the verge of blossoming.

Those who are beyond adolescent behavior, no matter how old they are and whether or not they are incarnate, could be said to be taking a parental role because they are capable of offering guidance and perspective. They seek to help neutralize the destructiveness.

Many people on a spiritual path are quite sensitive and feel keenly the raucousness of the adolescent carryings-on around them. Partly for this reason, they sometimes wish not to be on the physical plane any longer or pray that their present life be their last so that they do not "have to come back." Instead of seeing yourself as a victim of this unpleasantness, trying to escape it or insulate yourself from it, you might instead see yourself as a parent or older sibling seeking to offer support. Wise parents give their children space to go through what they need to but also are there to provide love and a good example.

We are not suggesting that if you are on a spiritual path, you are superior to those who are not and should condescend to those "unenlightened, adolescent" people. Every soul is on its own, equally valid path. However, those who are consciously more aware of what is going on, to whatever extent, can provide a stabilizing influence. You are a part of humanity and can contribute whatever enlightenment you possess to the whole. Because the need is so great at this time, your contributions are especially valuable.

Earth is in crisis. Since you are incarnate, you are experiencing that crisis. You are incarnate because you have chosen to be. It is unproductive to complain about it. The hallmark of someone truly on the path is that he takes responsibility for his choices, including being born. It was an act of courage to incarnate during this crisis. You are not alone in your efforts. There are many others, both incarnate and not, who are working to help.

If you make a statement in your life that says, "I am a positive, constructive force. I choose to be here, roll up my sleeves, and get to work," you help counter the destructive elements in the adolescent consciousness prevalent at this time. If your dominant statement in life is, "Get me out of here as fast as you can!" you are withdrawing your energy from the world and are doing less to counter these elements. Rolling up your sleeves is working with what is at hand, healing yourself and offering what you can to others in ways that benefit both you and them.

You can be happy while on the physical plane. You have not sentenced yourself to misery simply by reason of being here. Let's make another analogy: You decide to take a camping trip, and you are going to "rough it." You load yourself up with your backpack and sleeping bag. Backpacks can be heavy but are necessary if you are going to be well-supplied. There are times when the sun is hot and you feel drained from its ceaseless beating down upon you. There are other times when the temperature drops precipitously and you are cold. There are sometimes steep rocks in your way that must be climbed. You may fall. And so forth. From these remarks, you might think, if you have never done it, "Why would anyone go camping?" Why *do* people go camping? Some go for the opportunity to be outdoors and in touch with the elements, seeing magnificent scenery. Others relish the chance to test themselves in meeting challenges.

You are on a camping expedition. When it is done, you may say, "It is good to be home and get a shower and some decent food other than trail mix." But if you camped well, you will also have a sense of accomplishment.

MEDITATION

Take a moment to explore your commitment to being on the physical plane, and decide what it is you would most like to contribute during this crisis. State it in one sentence, if possible.

22 ❧ PIONEERING NEW IMAGES OF REALITY

Your ability to experience ecstasy or any other state of being depends on your ability to imagine its existence, and the space you have within to receive it. In fact, you experience any state—ecstasy, hell, or something in between (which is the case for most people)—because of your ability to imagine it and receive it into yourself. Most people have had abundant practice imagining and receiving states that are not entirely enjoyable. That is all right. But perhaps it can now be seen that this mechanism is indeed at work.

To imagine is to make images. There are many kinds of images. There are mental images (beliefs) and feeling images (emotions). Of course, there are visual images (pictures), and aural images (sounds) as well. Your faculty of imagination includes all these ways of imaging, and more.

Each person has a composite image of reality, the gestalt of his individual images that determines how he experiences reality. This image does not change very quickly, as a rule, on the physical plane. If it did, you would spend much of your time disoriented. It is good that it changes gradually, no more quickly than you are able to integrate. On higher planes, one's image changes more quickly, partly because of the practice that occurs on the physical plane, the densest of the seven planes. To learn how to do something fast, you must first master doing it slowly. On the physical plane, you have the opportunity to process each component of your image so that you can see what it is and make choices about it.

If you wish to know what your image of reality presently is, all you need to do is examine what your life looks like. Your life is a reflection of it. All the changes you make in your life are ultimately changes in that image.

Why is it that those who possess vivid imaginations are often unstable? There is sometimes an ability to change images more quickly than those changes can be assimilated.

Extreme cases of this can result in mental disorders. The mind, which is the part of self that makes sense of existence, cannot keep up. On the other hand, an ability to imagine vividly is a requisite for creativity, including channeling. If a channel is excessively limited in his ability to imagine, we who are channeled are restricted in what we are able to bring forth.

Those artists who are capable of bringing forth works of great impact—who can imagine something quite different from what most people imagine, and thereby bring change into the world—are often themselves unable to integrate those images and are therefore in difficult straits. Their willingness to go out on a limb is an enormous service to the rest of humanity, a gift that is usually not much appreciated at the time. In fact, those whose work is most radical are often those who are most rejected. Only after their deaths are they usually recognized. Why is this? Perhaps it takes the rest of humankind thirty, fifty, or a hundred years to integrate the new images to the point at which they can be appreciated—at least, that has been the case in the past. The lag time is decreasing now.

Your interest in this material indicates that you are developing the ability to imagine in new ways, putting yourself out on a limb to some degree. Maybe you have trouble explaining to others what you are doing. Maybe you have difficulty coping with this yourself, yet you could not stay within your old image. You are like a baby chick that has to peck its way out of its shell.

This pioneering willingness is of great import for humanity. Someone has to be first to imagine in a new way. New images are desperately needed if the human race is to survive. It was not that long ago that those who imaged a world free from pollution, for example, were almost universally considered to be fanatics, enemies of progress, a threat to economic well-being, and so forth. Because of those who even falteringly brought forth new images, today such

PIONEERING NEW IMAGES OF REALITY

an image is becoming more acceptable. Images have a way of expanding, like a seed that sprouts and begins to take root. A seed is a good analogy because it contains the image of what it wishes to grow. Inside an acorn is an image of an oak tree. Not every acorn brings forth an oak tree, but the potential is there. The image of a pollution-free world may not fully materialize. Older images may thwart the expansion of this image. It is not yet known what the outcome will be. No one can individually control the outcome on the mass level, but each person can nourish the expansion of new images within himself.

There are two basic images at play in humanity. One image is fear, the other is love. Fear has been a more potent image in the world than love for quite some time. Those who have sought to strengthen the image of love have been seen as naive (which they sometimes are), impractical and incapable of functioning in the world that is based on the image of fear. Those with an image of love have often been alone in the world and sometimes sadly persecuted. That, too, is finally beginning to change. Love as an image is no longer seen as being quite as unrealistic as it once was. We are not, of course, speaking of romantic love specifically, which may or may not be in the true image of love. We are speaking of agape, love that seeks the highest and greatest well-being of all.

New images are not always in focus. Pioneers are often not capable of seeing clearly what is ahead, but the courage it takes to move almost blindly into the unknown can be appreciated later. In whatever ways you are pioneering, it is essential to maintain your sense of purpose. Not many people will tell you how important and wonderful your efforts are. If others could see that this is the case, you would not be pioneering. The only ones who could have eyes to see this are those who have gone as far or farther. Therefore, do not excessively doubt yourself. If you do not adequately believe in what you are doing, you will hesitate on your path.

Self-doubt is the shadow of every pioneer. If you know this, you can keep it in perspective and keep moving forward. You will make mistakes—that is guaranteed. If only those who made no mistakes had self-confidence, there would be no progress.

You are the final authority on what you are doing in life. If you put too much emphasis on what others have to say about your life, you feed self-doubt. Certainly we are all in this together and have valuable pointers to give one another. It is smart to receive them and use them as they can be used. But any explorer will tell you that the key is to keep moving.

If you discover that you have been going around in circles, you found that out more quickly if you continued moving than had you stayed in the same place too long debating which way to go. Almost everyone has better results in life by continuing to move. Movement brings rhythm. Adjustments can be more easily made when there is movement. The paradox here is that it is easier to find inner stillness if you are moving: making choices, taking stands, and doing what you can see to do when much of what is ahead looks dark. We are not suggesting that you impulsively jump into things, making decisions that you are not ready to make. There is a balance here. But all too many get stuck out of fear. There comes a time to move. When that time comes, if you do not move, you will feel increasingly uncomfortable.

You do not have to change your old image entirely, even if you know that it is inadequate. You only have to take one step forward. That will lead to another step. As you move, your new image becomes clearer—of course, because you are getting closer to it. If you stubbornly refuse to move, your new image becomes increasingly theoretical, abstract, and unrealistic. It is only by moving closer and closer to it that you can hone it, clarify it, and bring it in with greater strength and accuracy.

PIONEERING NEW IMAGES OF REALITY

During the past week, I did a series of drawings of battle scenes. I found myself getting a great charge out of doing scenes of people firing on each other, horses charging, and so on. In fact, I saw some brilliant lights emanating at times. Afterwards, I became frightened because of the implications of the destructiveness that I identified with. I don't know how to reconcile the idea of agape with my seeming love toward this destructiveness.

You are getting in touch with old images so that they can be released. You cannot move into new images until you see clearly the old ones. Otherwise, the old and the new images try to cancel each other out. Only those who have enough perspective to see the old can venture into the new.

Should I investigate this desire for destruction even further?

Allow to come up whatever is seeking to come up. You mentioned that you also saw a light. This is indication that these old images are coming to light. That is positive movement.

MEDITATION

Listen for a moment to your heart. Ask that your heart bring forth agape. Create for yourself a visual image of agape. May your image manifest in the larger, shared reality of human existence.

23 ❦ BEAUTY

The Earth is a very beautiful planet. Every planet has its points, but Earth, even after being mutilated by pollution and other forms of destruction, retains extraordinary loveliness. We are not limiting this to just what is commonly called nature, but would include almost everything.

It is worthwhile to notice the beauty of the earth as you move through your days. Can you find the beauty in a subway station? We are not suggesting that you close your eyes to what is not beautiful, but if that is all you are seeing, you are not seeing the whole. What is beautiful deserves at least equal time in your awareness. If you concentrate on what is ugly, you are magnifying ugliness, especially if you have charged feelings about it.

A good place to notice beauty is when you are shopping for food. Are not fruits and vegetables beautiful? Someone who is gifted at seeing beauty could spend much time looking at a head of cabbage, finding much to appreciate in it. One definition of an artist is someone who can see things in the commonplace that elude others. When we use the word "see," we are not limiting it to physical vision; we include hearing beauty, smelling beauty, and so forth, in addition to perception of the nonphysical.

The more you appreciate the beauty that is, the more you will act to increase beauty within your domain. One whose home is beautiful, no matter what her budget is, is usually one with an ability to see beauty.

A great lesson of life is making choices. The more you see, the more selections you have to choose from. If you see beauty, you can choose beauty. To make an analogy, if you are colorblind, you are more limited in being able to create beautiful combinations of colors than if you can discern colors. The ability to see beauty is itself an analogy for a larger truth. The ability to see anything at all allows you greater choice-making. When you do not see, you do not know what your choices are or even that you have choices.

If you are a sensitive person, you have the capacity to pick up impressions that might elude others. A radio that is sensitive can pick up signals that another radio cannot. Sometimes people are considered to be too sensitive because they are easily hurt. In such a case, a person is sensitive or tuned in to those things that can hurt—that is what is being picked up. This indicates an aspect of self that is seeking to be healed. But sensitivity is not necessarily the ability to be hurt. Full-spectrum sensitivity allows one to receive information from all directions, internally and externally. A person who is sensitive in this respect does not need to be hit over the head to get the message, whatever it is.

Often people are sensitive in some areas and insensitive in others. If you have extensive experience in a particular area, you are more sensitive in that area. If you are a musician, you are likely to be sensitive to subtleties in music, whereas if you are an architect, you are probably sensitive to fine points in the architecture you view. If you have done a lot of work with the relationships in your life, you will tend to notice things in relationships that might escape others.

No one can be an expert in every field, but the more alert you are in your life, the more sensitivity you can develop. You could say that your life largely consists of what you are sensitive to. You have learned about those things and have developed the ability to handle them skillfully. The result of developing sensitivity in any area is being able to discern the beauty in it. Almost anyone can be moved by a beautiful piece of music. Nevertheless, one who is expert in music can be lifted to a higher experience than one who cannot really discern what is there, all other things being equal.

However, experts sometimes lose the ability to appreciate beauty unless something is, in their view, flawless. A person who can appreciate an expensive bottle of wine may no longer enjoy one that is not expensive. This is understandable, yet ideally he would not lose his ability to enjoy any pleasant qualities the inexpensive wine might possess. It is not that he would ignore its weaknesses, but that he would appreciate it for what it is.

Everything has its points. Everything has at least some beauty. It may constitute a minuscule portion, but it is there. If you are constantly in judgment of yourself, emphasizing what is wrong or ugly about you, you will also tend to see the world in this way. You might ask what was beautiful in Adolf Hitler. Not much, but how often do you come across such an extreme?

The more you appreciate beauty, the more you can draw beauty into your life. It is wise to deliberately bring things into your life that have beauty you can appreciate. Perhaps treating yourself to fresh flowers on a regular basis would do it for you, or having some clothing you find beautiful, or a work of art. If you do avail yourself of these things, take time to really see and identify with them. If you marvel at a bouquet of roses, you are ultimately marveling at a quality in yourself.

You are a part of all, and everything is in you. You cannot appreciate anything that you have not yet discovered in yourself. If you recognize beauty in other people, you are reminding yourself of your own beauty. If you find only fault in other people, you are reminding yourself of your own shortcomings. It is wise to be aware of your shortcomings, but becoming obsessed with them leads nowhere. Strive to have a more beautiful experience of life each day. This happens not through battling your shortcomings but through increasing beauty. If you recognize, for example, impatience at work in you, increase the beauty of patience rather than increasing your dissatisfaction with yourself.

MEDITATION

Close your eyes and imagine the most beautiful thing you can. First see it before you. Then become part of it.

Now that you have at least one image of what represents beauty for you, think of something you could do to bring more beauty into your life. If your image was that of a waterfall, it might be to meditate on that image. It might be literally to visit a waterfall, or to find a picture of one you like and put it up where you can see it often.

Beauty is a manifestation of love. Love is all there is. That which lacks beauty is lacking in love, or lacking in being; it is only partial rather than whole. If people were not equipped with the ability to recognize beauty, they would have no capacity to expand love or to grow into agape. Since agape is the name of the game, it is necessary equipment.

Each planet is designed with a particular lesson or experiment in mind. The lessons of many other planets are simpler than those of Earth; therefore, the beauty is a simpler beauty than what is found here. The earth is a special experiment. It is a place where balanced diversity is sought. Therefore, there is more variety of animal, plant, and mineral forms than on many other planets. There is no such thing as an ugly planet, but the more complexity there is, the more depth the beauty can have. A simple poem expressing an honest sentiment can be quite beautiful, but a complex and beautiful poem can bring beauty to a greater depth. Music is another analogy: a simple melody is potentially quite beautiful, but a symphony can express a higher beauty if it is in harmony with love. On the other hand, if a symphony's complexity clouds or complicates its potential beauty rather than elevating it, a simple melody that clearly reveals its beauty is more beautiful. There is nothing in its natural state that is not beautiful. An amoeba is beautiful, but the human form, being far more complex than an amoeba, has much greater depth of potential beauty.

There is great beauty on every level of your being. Your essence is beautiful beyond your ability to imagine. As you learn to see and feel the beauty that is present and available

BEING IN THE WORLD

everywhere, your life becomes beautiful and full of love.

EPILOGUE

The world as you experience it reflects your beliefs about it and about yourself. Love yourself and you cannot help but love the world. Love the world and you act in such a way that the world reflects your love back to you. Believe that the world is generous, and you naturally receive its generosity. Keep a clear vision of what you wish to create, and you use your resources, inner and outer, to create it.

You do not need to accept that anything stated here is true. You do not, by the same token, need to decide that it is false. Instead, you can see if these concepts are of use to you. One's understanding of reality is rightly constantly shifting. If you see the world tomorrow in the same way you do today, you are not living fully. If we have stimulated you to open yourself to new ways of seeing, we are pleased.

BACK MATTER

ABOUT THE AUTHOR

SHEPHERD HOODWIN has been channeling since 1986. He also does intuitive readings, mediumship, past-life regression, healing, counseling, and channeling coaching (teaching others to channel). He has conducted workshops on the Michael teachings throughout the United States and Europe.

    Shepherd is a graduate of the University of Oregon. He lives in Laguna Niguel, California.

https://shepherdhoodwin.com

TWITTER:
@shepherdh
@EnlightenNitwit

FACEBOOK:
https://www.facebook.com/shepherd.hoodwin
https://www.facebook.com/shepherd.hoodwin.author/
https://www.facebook.com/JourneyOfYourSoul/
https://www.facebook.com/EnlightenmentforNitwits/

shepherdhoodwin@gmail.com

Summerjoy Press
99 Pearl
Laguna Niguel CA 92677-4818

GLOSSARY

Agape: A state of unconditional love for everything. This is considered the highest goal.

Astral plane: Where we go between lifetimes and when we are finished with the physical plane.

Causal plane: The next plane after the astral. Michael's plane of creation.

Essence: Soul, or higher self, in distinction to the outer personality, or lower self.

False personality: False ego, the part of self motivated by fear.

Overleaves: Seven types of personality traits that "overlay" the essence, chosen to facilitate the purposes of the lifetime.

Physical plane: The densest of the seven planes, where we presently reside.

Planes of creation: Physical, astral, causal, akashic, mental, messianic, and buddhaic. Just as there are seven colors in the rainbow and seven steps in a musical scale, each with a different vibratory rate, there are seven levels of being on the spectrum of existence. The slowest speed of vibration is on the physical plane; the highest, on the buddhaic plane. From there, universal substance returns to the Tao.

Role: One of the seven types of essences: *server, priest, artisan, sage, warrior, king,* and *scholar*. Everyone has a particular role. It defines one's way of being or fundamental style, not one's worldly position.

Soul: Essence, or higher self, in distinction to the outer personality, or lower self.

Tao: The All That Is. Usually refers to the dimensionless ground of being rather than to its expression in the seven planes of creation of the manifest universe. Michael normally uses the word *Tao* in place of *God* (depending on the beliefs of those listening) because God is usually personified and tends to connote something hierarchical and judgmental. They also sometimes use the word God to signify the highest or overall consciousness of our manifest universe.

OTHER BOOKS BY SHEPHERD HOODWIN

Available at https://shepherdhoodwin.com/book/

All Is Choice

Few realize how profound, multi-faceted, and far-reaching the concept of choice is in our spiritual growth. This short book explores topics such as what is and is not our right to choose, our power as creators and the limits of our reality creation, how consciousness expands, and much more.

Compassion for Evil
A Metaphysical View

Compassion for Evil explores the nature of evil from the soul's point of view, and how we can skillfully deal with it as lightworkers.

Embracing What Is
Spiritual Keys to Happiness

This book is an abridged version of *Happiness and the Michael Teachings*, without technical Michael teachings terminology. A free version is available at Smashwords.com.

Energy Literacy
How to Perceive and Take Charge of Your Spiritual Well-Being

Energy Literacy is an introduction to how to perceive our energy field and release negativity. Topics include chakras, contracts, vows, cording, entities, implants, psychic attack, earthbound souls, soul retrieval, and more.

Enlightenment for Nitwits
The Complete Guide

BEING IN THE WORLD

This hilarious metaphysical/self-help humor collection will appeal to Oprah and Dave Barry fans as well as those with more esoteric interests. In a style reminiscent of comedian Steven Wright, it's full of wry one-liners along with longer, hilariously mind-bending pieces on a wide range of subjects, tied together by the idea of clueless humans trying to find enlightenment.

"I love *Enlightenment for Nitwits*! It is the funniest book I have read in several decades. If laughter leads to enlightenment, it will certainly do it. Nothing—thank God—is sacred in this delightful spoof on life in general."
—C. Norman Shealy, M.D., author of *Life Beyond 100*

Growing Through Joy

This thought-provoking book explores the nature of personal growth.

Happiness and the Michael Teachings
Learning to Embrace What Is

Happiness is the ultimate goal of every spiritual teaching. Here we explore several principles of what the Michael teachings refer to as growing through joy.

Healing the Gut
A Crib Sheet for Eliminating SIBO

This short book offers tips for those with digestive problems and related diseases, focusing on the Specific Carbohydrate Diet.

Journey of Your Soul
A Channel Explores the Michael Teachings

This is the most in-depth discussion of the Michael teachings to date. It may also be the first analytical study of channeling written by a channel. It has forewords by John Friedlander, co-author of *Psychic Psychology*, and Jon Klimo, author of *Channeling: Investigations on Receiving Information from Paranormal Sources*. Klimo writes, "*Journey of Your Soul* may well be the best (Michael) book of them all due to its clarity, thoroughness, and detail, and thanks to the fact that the author, an exceptionally clear-headed Michael channel himself, brings real integrity and authenticity to our understanding of Michael in particular and to the channeling process in general."

Loving from Your Soul
Creating Powerful Relationships

This inspiring, transformative book explores the nature of love itself as well as practical matters of relationships. One reader wrote, "There are phrases that are so inspiring that I wrote them down to refer to when I need them. I am looking forward to reading this book again and again."

Meditations for Self-Discovery
Guided Journeys for Communicating with Your Inner Self

This is a beautiful collection of forty-five vivid, often pastoral, guided imagery meditations channeled from Shepherd's essence. There are many meditation recordings available, but this is one of the first collections of meditations in book form that can be read to oneself or others. Teachers and group leaders would find it particularly useful.

Opening to Healing

This uplifting book explores the spiritual aspect of healing.

Unconditional Love in Politics
Or Have You Hugged a Republican/Democrat Today?

Is unconditional love in politics an oxymoron? Thus far, it's been a rare commodity if it's ever been there. This book explores what you can do about it, as well as why both right and left have useful parts to play in our evolution, the factors that influence a person's tilt to the right or left, and what unconditional love might look like in this sphere.

Why We're Attracted
Spiritual, Psychological and Physical Elements That Draw Us to Others

Just why are we attracted to some people and not to others? This book explores a multitude of factors on three levels: spiritual, psychological, and physical. Topics include agreements, life path, soul chemistry, male/female energy ratio, celibacy, body-type attraction, sexual orientation, monogamy, and polyfidelity.

REVIEWS

I absolutely love this book. It was precisely what I needed to hear. There is so much helpful insight in it.

Food for the soul. The clarity and intuitive veracity contained lifts the mind toward transcendent beauty.

A really lovely book that made me feel a lot better.

I was immediately moved.

Every time I opened it up to read a chapter, it addressed the exact situation I was going through. I felt like it was personally speaking to me, to the point that I laughed out loud at the coincidences after a while. This book will resonate with people nearly universally.

There is a lot of wise advice.

A welcome addition to any spiritual library. It shows how true spiritual growth comes from living in the world with all of its messy human realities, and provides a realistic road map for how to be a "spiritual being having a human experience." Well written and easy to read

If you have not read Mr. Hoodwin's other books, its time to snuggle up and read them. A fast and easy read.

I recommend this to anyone on a spiritual path or simply looking for meaning and purpose in their life.

This is a work of beauty, a gift of wisdom, and an invitation to rise and shine.

Printed in Great Britain
by Amazon